Getting Infrastructure Right

A FRAMEWORK FOR BETTER GOVERNANCE

This work is published under the responsibility of the Secretary-General of the OECD. The opinions expressed and arguments employed herein do not necessarily reflect the official views of OECD member countries.

This document and any map included herein are without prejudice to the status of or sovereignty over any territory, to the delimitation of international frontiers and boundaries and to the name of any territory, city or area.

Please cite this publication as:
OECD (2017), *Getting Infrastructure Right: A framework for better governance*, OECD Publishing, Paris.
http://dx.doi.org/10.1787/9789264272453-en

ISBN 978-92-64-27244-6 (print)
ISBN 978-92-64-27245-3 (PDF)

Photo credits: Cover © Jeffrey Fisher

Foreword

Infrastructure has always been difficult to get right. Apart from the technical challenges, poor governance of infrastructure is a major reason why infrastructure projects fail to meet their timeframe, budget, and service delivery objectives. *Getting Infrastructure Right: a Framework for Better Governance* lays out practical governance tools to help policy makers improve the management of infrastructure policy from strategic planning to project-level delivery.

The report is composed of three chapters: The challenges in infrastructure governance; the framework itself, built around ten key dimensions of an effective infrastructure policy system; and an overview of current practices in infrastructure governance based on a comprehensive OECD Survey of 27 countries. The ten key dimensions relate to how governments prioritise, plan, budget, deliver, regulate and evaluate infrastructure investment and can be used to evaluate the quality of a country's infrastructure governance. The framework emphasises that successful governance of infrastructure depends on a coherent strategic planning process, an open and transparent prioritisation mechanism and decision processes based on affordability and cost efficiency, a clear regulatory and institutional framework, robust co-ordination across levels of governments and evaluation mechanisms that monitor performance throughout the life cycle of the asset.

The report is an update and extension of OECD (2015) "Towards a Framework for the Governance of Infrastructure," which was welcomed by the OECD Ministerial Council Meeting, 3-4 June 2015, in Paris, France, and at the G20 Finance Ministers and Central Bank Governors Meeting, 4-5 September 2015 in Ankara, Turkey.

This work was carried out by the OECD Public Governance and Territorial Development Directorate (GOV) and is the result of close co-operation across divisions and contributions from a wide range of expertise under the direction of Rolf Alter, Jón R. Blöndal and Andrew Davies. Ian Hawkesworth led the work and was one of the authors together with Juliane Jansen. Substantial contributions were received from Dorothée Allain-Dupré, Rüdiger Ahrend, Abel Schumann (regional development and co-ordination across levels of government), Céline Kauffmann, Filippo Cavassini, Mark McLeish, Anna Pietikainen (regulatory design), Alessandro Bellatoni, Craig Matasick (consultation and stakeholder engagement), Matthieu Cahen, Kenza Khachani (public procurement and infrastructure delivery), Frédéric St-Martin (integrity and corruption threats), Jack Radish (managing systematic risk), and Dejan Makovšek (private sector participation). Valuable comments were provided by Juan Garin and Camila Vammalle. We thank Bonifacio Agapin, Kate Lancaster and Andrea Uhrhammer for their help preparing the document for publication.

The framework benefited greatly from the support and inputs provided by the OECD Network of Senior Infrastructure Officials, who identified the principal objective of policy in each area and provided most of the data.

Table of contents

Tables

Figures

Executive Summary

Infrastructure is one of the backbones of both *productivity* and *inclusiveness:* Firms derive much of their competitive edge from their ability to use modern infrastructures, while societies depend on good infrastructure to ensure equal opportunity and *equal access to services* for citizens. Nevertheless, infrastructure has always been difficult to get right. Apart from the technical challenges, poor governance of infrastructure is a major reason why infrastructure projects fail to meet their timeframe, budget, and service delivery objectives.

Substantial benefits can be realised by better governance of public infrastructure. This report presents a Framework for the Governance of Infrastructure that countries can use to assess the adequacy of their infrastructure management systems. The Framework covers ten key dimensions relating to how governments prioritise, plan, budget, deliver, regulate and evaluate infrastructure investment. Substantive work by the OECD Network of Senior Infrastructure and PPP Officials has identified the principal objective of policy in each area:

1. Establish a national long-term strategic vision that addresses infrastructure service needs

2. Manage the integrity and corruption threats at all stages of the process, from project conception to delivery

3. Establish clear criteria to guide the choice of delivery mode (PPP vs direct public provision, etc.)

4. Ensure good regulatory design and maintain a predictable regulatory framework for investment.

5. Integrate a consultation process early enough so that decisions benefit from real stakeholder engagement

6. Co-ordinate infrastructure policy across levels of government in such a way that investment decisions by central and subnational governments are coherent

7. Guard affordability and value for money by using and applying cost-benefit and other methods rigorously and consistently

8. Generate, analyse and disclose useful data to increase transparency and ensure accountability

9. Integrate mechanisms to evaluate the performance of assets throughout their lifecycle

10. Review existing infrastructure resilience in the face of evolving natural and man-made risks and develop guidelines to future proof new infrastructures.

An analysis of current practices in OECD member and non-member countries shows that for some dimensions good practices are common, while other practices suggested by the framework are less present and demand attention.

A deficit can be identified, for example, with respect to **long term planning, prioritisation and co-ordination** practices. While most countries have sectoral plans, this silo approach can make it difficult to achieve cross sectoral policy objectives such as regional development or adaptation to climate change and can miss chances for synergies between sectors such as energy, transport, housing and urban development.

Co-ordination of investment across levels of government is another area where more effort is required. Roles and responsibilities among different government entities are often unclear, capacities and skills at lower levels of government are sometimes weak, and co-ordination mechanisms, including mentoring, are insufficient.

It can be difficult to monitor the **performance** of infrastructure and maintain value for money through the lifecycle of the asset. Most institutions are responsible for the development and delivery of infrastructure, not for 'after sales service'. Although the preparation and construction phases inevitably require the majority of resources, responsibility for the assessment and monitoring of projects over the following decade or more of its lifespan needs to be clearly allocated. Currently, performance assessment for example is only mandated in half of the countries and audits by the Supreme Audit Institution (SAI) regarding infrastructure assets are mainly conducted on a case by case basis.

Pressure to give voice to citizens and stakeholders is reflected by widely used mandatory **consultation processes.** However, consultation takes place mainly during the project preparation phase, i.e., after the discussion on infrastructure strategy, needs and options has been completed.

As many actors in the public and private sectors can be vulnerable to **integrity risk** in infrastructure projects, a whole of government approach is essential to effectively address these risks. Most OECD countries have an explicit policy in place that regulates conflicts of interest in the tender panel, as well as formal appeal mechanisms in the tendering process. However, specific measures against corruption and integrity threats in infrastructure are only applied in half of the countries.

Governments must ensure that infrastructure projects are **affordable** and that the overall investment envelope is sustainable. Value for money is generally assessed using a combination of quantitative (such as cost/benefit analysis) and qualitative tools that seek to establish the overall societal return on investment. However, in many countries, this assessment is used on a case by case basis rather than systematically.

A constraint for clear decision making and evaluation is the **lack of data**. There is a lack of systematic data-collection regarding the cost and performance of infrastructure assets. While many countries do collect data, most of the data that would be required to compare the overall costs of projects financed through various alternative mechanisms is not systematically collected, processed or disclosed. As such, the real cost of many infrastructure assets and the return on the original investment are very opaque.

Chapter 1

Infrastructure governance challenges

Infrastructure has always been difficult to get right. Apart from the technical challenges, poor governance of infrastructure is a major reason why infrastructure projects fail to meet their timeframe, budget, and service delivery objectives. This chapter highlights the current challenges that policy makers are facing today, including the lack of leadership, well defined areas of responsibility and pipeline prioritisation; unstable regulatory frameworks and weak institutional capacity across levels of government; political and social opposition, as well as high vulnerability to corruption, capture and financial mismanagement at all stages of the infrastructure governance cycle.

Infrastructure represents a governance challenge

OECD analysis has shown that substantial benefits can be realised by better governance of public investment throughout its life-cycle and that the quality of public governance of public investment is linked to growth outcomes at the national and subnational levels (OECD, 2013a) as well as good budgetary governance (OECD, 2015b). Several recent studies (OECD, 2015a; OECD, 2013a; OECD, 2013b; IMF, 2015; WB, 2014) estimate that improvement in infrastructure management could lead to substantial savings and enhanced infrastructure productivity. The objective of good infrastructure governance is to make the right projects happen in a manner that is cost efficient, affordable, and trusted by users and citizens. The elements and contours of a national governance framework for infrastructure are set out in this document.

Conversely, poor governance is a major reason why infrastructure projects fail to meet their timeframe, budget, and service delivery objectives. The challenges are also similar if not greater in developing countries, where infrastructure investment accounts for a higher share of GDP and institutional frameworks are less mature. The answer to this challenge demands a strengthening of the entire institutional architecture of government in order to deliver the right strategic infrastructure on time, within budget, and in a manner that commands the confidence of all stakeholders. It raises questions such as how the public sector should prioritise, plan, budget, assess, deliver, regulate infrastructure.

By the governance of infrastructure is meant the processes, tools, and norms of interaction, decision-making, and monitoring used by governmental organisations and their counterparts with respect to making infrastructure services available to public and private users, including citizens (See Annex C for a description if infrastructure delivery).

The initial paper this document builds on was welcomed by the OECD Ministerial Council Meeting, 3-4 June 2015, in Paris, France, and at the G20 Finance Ministers and Central Bank Governors Meeting, 4-5 September 2015 in Ankara, Turkey. A list of key relevant OECD Recommendations that inform this work can be found in Annex A.

Strategies, institutions and values need to be aligned

Regardless of how public infrastructure services are delivered, there are a number of challenges, discussed below, that all countries face.

Designing a strategic vision is crucial but difficult. A necessary condition for a successful infrastructure programme is appropriate strategic planning that sets a long term vision for the where the country should be in, say, 20 years and what infrastructure are needed. This requires identifying what investment should be undertaken and determining essential components, needs, and trade-offs and how they should be prioritised – across sectors, projects and regions. However, the many dimensions of infrastructure governance, as discussed below, make this difficult to do.

Infrastructure projects are vulnerable to corruption, capture and mismanagement throughout the infrastructure cycle. The size of the projects, their technical complexity and the multiplicity of stakeholders involved in the infrastructure cycle make them particularly prone to corruption, capture and mismanagement. As noted in The OECD Foreign Bribery Report (OECD, 2014a) two-thirds of all foreign bribery cases occurred in four sectors related to infrastructure; extractive (19%), construction (15%), transport and storage (15%) and information and communication (10%).

Without well-managed consultation good projects may falter. Involving stakeholders such as users, civil society organisations, and the private sector can improve legitimacy, project quality, and ultimately the effectiveness of the asset. Stakeholder involvement can establish a shared vision for development, improve the assessment of investment needs and of the environmental and social sustainability of the project, reveal the importance of cross-border linkages, strengthen trust in government, and cultivate support and adherence for specific investment projects.

Co-ordination across levels of government is difficult. Sub-national governments often play a leading role in infrastructure investment, and infrastructure assets' impact oftentimes does not follow jurisdictional lines, intergovernmental co-ordination is important. However, regional preferences do not always easily align with national ones and intra-regional rivalries may pose a challenge to co-ordination. Therefore, better public investment co-ordination and governance can materially boost investment outcomes (OECD, 2013a; OECD, 2014a).

Uncertainty with regards to revenue flows and sources can erode confidence in a project's affordability. Long-term financial sustainability can be an important challenge in infrastructure sectors that rely on user charges, in particular water, energy, and to some extent transport. Evidence shows that tariff-setting is a very difficult task and can be a highly political endeavour. This can make investors reluctant to invest.

Unstable regulatory frameworks and political systems can prevent long-term decisions. The instability or lack of credibility of institutions in charge of regulating infrastructure development and management as well as burdensome and frequent changes in the political system and consequent regulatory framework will increase the sense of risk for project developers.

A political jurisdiction and an infrastructure asset's functional area are often not the same. Since the efficient scale of the asset often exceeds the boundaries of individual regions or localities (OECD, 2014a) horizontal co-ordination across jurisdictions is essential to increase the most value and affordability of the investment.

Weak institutional capacity undermines project development. As part of the prioritisation of projects and then detailed project preparation a number of studies are carried out with increasing degrees of accuracy e.g. the demand for the infrastructure service, the cost of the asset and environmental impact assessments as well as cost/benefit analysis. This then serves as the basis for the project development. This has proven difficult to do well in a number of cases. This can be because of a lack of organisational, technical, commercial skills, co-ordination and experience, and the process can at times be forced due to political pressures, which leads to a - probably more expensive - scope change. In the end, this may result in an expensive contract, a failed bidding or (if relevant) a project unable to attract private financing.

A lack of systematic data collection on performance undermines evidence based decision making and disclosure of key information. Countries should carefully assess which delivery modality (e.g. public works, PPP, etc.) is likely to yield the most value for money. Good practice requires the use of comprehensive cost-benefit techniques and a robust assurance process, which may be challenging due to a lack of systematic data. Presently very few countries systematically collect and use financial and non-financial data from various types of infrastructure investments.

Allocating risks between public and private parties can be difficult. Many projects flounder due to a misalignment between what private sector partners will accept in terms of risk and the expectations of some public sector entities. The public sector should only transfer those risks which the private side is better suited to manage. For instance, as noted above, the private sector will usually be more suited to handle commercial risks than the public sector, whereas the opposite is usually the case with respect to legal and political risks.

Institutional incentives may generate suboptimal investment choices. At times, projects may be chosen for reasons other than maximising cost effectiveness. Motivations might include a wish to capitalise on an existing subsidy or a wish to finance the asset in a non-transparent manner off the government's balance sheet by using, for example, a PPP.

Infrastructure projects are vulnerable to corruption, capture and mismanagement throughout the infrastructure cycle. The size of the projects, their technical complexity and the multiplicity of stakeholders involved in the infrastructure cycle make them particularly prone to corruption, capture and mismanagement. As noted in The OECD Foreign Bribery Report (OECD, 2014b) two-thirds of all foreign bribery cases occurred in four sectors highly related to infrastructure; extractive (19%), construction (15%), transport and storage (15%) and information and communication (10%).

Political dynamics may undermine sound decision-making with regards to infrastructure. Related to the above point, the prioritisation of public investment needs is particularly prone to capture and grand corruption. Stakeholders involved at that stage may be tempted to push for or reject infrastructure projects that would primarily benefit or protect their own private or political interests. In the same manner, the electoral cycle may prompt governments to push projects forward that should not have been prioritised.

Bibliography

IMF (2015), "Making Public Investment More Efficient", Staff Report prepared by IMF staff and completed on June 11, International Monetary Fund (IMF), Washington, D.C.

OECD (2013a), Investing Together: Working Effectively Across Levels of Government, OECD Publishing, Paris, http://dx.doi.org/10.1787/9789264197022-en

OECD (2013b), G20/OECD High-level principles of long term investment financing by Institutional investors, www.oecd.org/finance/private-pensions/G20-OECD-Principles-LTI-Financing.pdf

OECD (2014a), Recommendation of the Council on Effective Public Investment Across Levels of Government, OECD Publishing, Paris, www.oecd.org/gov/regional-policy/recommendation-effective-public-investment-across-levels-of-government.htm

OECD (2014b), OECD Foreign Bribery Report: An Analysis of the Crime of Bribery of Foreign Public Officials, OECD Publishing, Paris, http://dx.doi.org/10.1787/9789264226616-en

OECD (2015a), Towards a framework for the governance of Infrastructure, Paper welcomed at G20 Finance Ministers and Central Bank Governors Meeting 4-5 September 2015, Ankara, Turkey

OECD (2015b), *Governance of Water Regulators*, OECD Publishing, Paris, http://dx.doi.org/10.1787/9789264231092-en

World Bank (2014), "The Power of Public Investment Management: Transforming Resources into Assets for Growth", Directions in Development, Washington, D.C.

Chapter 2

A Framework for the Governance of Infrastructure

This chapter presents the ten dimensions of the framework for the governance of public infrastructure. The dimensions relate to how governments prioritise, plan, budget, deliver, regulate and evaluate infrastructure investment, and are based on substantive work by the OECD Network of Senior PPP and Infrastructure Officials. Each area covers the principal objective of policy in each area, followed by key questions decision makers need to address and indicators identifying the enabling factors.

Drawing on the extensive body of OECD instruments that address the issues raised above, we can identify a number of infrastructure governance dimensions that need to be addressed regardless of how the infrastructure service is provided. The dimensions can be more or less salient depending on the circumstances and can be addressed in a multiplicity of organisational and institutional models. Together they complement each other and together will form a strong enabling environment.

Below, each dimension is addressed at the outset with a normative recommendation followed by an explanatory section that ends in key questions decision maker needs to address and indicators identifying enabling factors. An overview of the policy dimensions and the relevant key policy questions and indicators can be found in Annex E.

1. Develop a strategic vision for infrastructure

Establish a national long-term strategic vision that addresses infrastructure service needs. Ideally the strategy should provide guidance on how the needs should be met, although there has to be room for adjustment as more information is gathered. The strategy should be politically sanctioned, co-ordinated across levels of government, take stakeholder views into account and be based on clear assumptions. It should also be aligned with spatial and land-use planning policies. If applicable, strategic planning for infrastructure projects should occur through the mechanisms that exist in the spatial planning system. Special procedures designed to circumvent the spatial and land use planning system should be avoided.

Definition

A long term national strategic vision is a politically sanctioned document that demands concrete action in terms of infrastructure services to society over the long term. This might go beyond a normal political mandate period. The design of the vision requires a process that distils complex and multi-faceted infrastructure issues, cutting across a multiplicity of actors, sectors and interests, into a coherent set of decisions with long term impact, including projects and processes. Such a process should be anchored in central agencies (Chief Executive, Finance, similar) have substantial input from policy departments, sub-national governments (see Dimension No. 5) and civil society, business stakeholders.

Why is this important?

A necessary condition for a successful infrastructure programme is appropriate strategic planning. This requires identifying what investment should be undertaken, determining the essential components, needs and trade-offs, and how they should be prioritised. Conversely, weak or insufficient planning often impedes their successful implementation and operation later in the project cycle. The reason why designing a clear and coherent strategic vision is difficult stems essentially from the complex nature of infrastructure investment.

- The infrastructure issue cuts across different institutions, jurisdictions, levels of government, policy areas and professional disciplines which makes it difficult to aggregate into a coherent view. Analysis tends to be done in silos reflecting the various stakeholders.

- Infrastructure development serves multiple objectives, with multiple policy goals such as growth, productivity, affordability, inclusive development, environmental objectives, potentially being in opposition.

- This is a period of significant economic, technological and climate change, and judging the right strategy is difficult and important

- Infrastructure requires space. To avoid conflicts over land use and incompatible land uses in close proximity, strategic planning for infrastructure should be closely co-ordinated with spatial and land use planning policies.

- Infrastructure not only requires space. Many infrastructure projects (in particular related to transport) also exert a strong influence on future land-use patterns. Strategic infrastructure planning should consider these effects and make sure they are aligned with the objectives of spatial and land-use plans.

- Infrastructure has long-term impact and gestation periods and requires predictability and sober analysis, but infrastructure is extremely sensitive to political and economic/business cycles that vary markedly over time.

- Some projects are large and have a long term budget: infrastructure planning needs to be attuned to the risk of over-investing generally or to a specific project.

- Good infrastructure planning requires identification of necessary complementarities across sectors. For example, investments in housing need to be complemented by the right investment in transport networks (OECD, 2014a).

Key policy questions

- Is there a whole of government vision for infrastructure investment in the medium to long term?

- Is there an established process for generating, monitoring and adjusting a national strategic infrastructure vision?

- Is there a dedicated unit or institution responsible for monitoring, generating, assessing, costing and creating debate around infrastructure policy?

- Are there appropriate tools and processes that link the allocation of public resources to the strategic infrastructure vision?

- Are strategic infrastructure plans aligned with existing spatial and land-use plans?

- Is strategic infrastructure planning integrated into the spatial planning process or does it rely on independent processes?

Indicators

- Presence of a long term strategic plan

- Strategic frameworks for public investment implementation

- Budget allocation to projects in plan

- Dedicated processes and units

- Inter-departmental or ministerial committees and platforms to design infrastructure strategies

2. Manage threats to integrity

Opportunities to derive illicit rents should be mitigated at each stage of the development of public infrastructure projects. As many actors in the public and private sectors can be vulnerable to integrity risk in infrastructure projects, a whole of government approach is essential to effectively address these risks.

Definition

OECD's 2016 Integrity Framework for Public Investment provides that corruption can occur not only through bribery but also through other behaviours that harm the public interest, such as undue influence on infrastructure decision-making processes, mismanagement and collusion. These behaviours can eventually lead to the capture of the whole infrastructure project. Corruption relates to the abuse of a position or office for private gain. Capture occurs when the interests of a narrow group dominate those of other stakeholders and the public. Mismanagement generally refers to the act of managing infrastructure projects, including associated public resources, dishonestly or incompetently. Collusion refers to combinations, conspiracies or agreements among sellers to raise or fix prices and to reduce output in order to increase profits.

Why is this important?

Corruption allegations often surround government-led infrastructure projects. The extent of public officials' discretion on the investment decision, the scale and complexity of the projects as well as the multiplicity of stages and stakeholders involved make infrastructure projects highly vulnerable to corruption. The Construction Sector Transparency Initiative (CoST) estimates that 10-30% of the investment in a publicly funded construction project may be lost through mismanagement and corruption (COST, 2012). Within the European Union, corruption costs are estimated to EUR 120 billion per year (European Commission, 2014). The OECD Foreign Bribery Report (2014h) also suggests that two-thirds of foreign bribery cases occurred in 4 sectors related to infrastructure: extractive (19%), construction (15%), transport and storage (15%) and information and communication (10%).

Added-value for the local or national economy, fiscal prudence, cost-effectiveness and resilience of infrastructure may be severely undermined when infrastructure projects are meant to unduly benefit inefficient economic actors and organised crime, or to disproportionately benefit political parties' or candidates' donors or core electoral base at the expense of society as a whole. Corruption can occur at every step of an infrastructure project, including the selection, appraisal, planning, tendering, implementation and monitoring phases (OECD, 2016).

As provided by the OECD Recommendation on Public Integrity, a whole of government, risk based approach is thus essential to effectively close the gaps through which elected and non-elected public officials, lobbyists, regulators, contractors, engineers, suppliers, trade unions and civil society organisations can abuse their position to derive illicit rents at the expense of the public interest (OECD, 2017). The OECD Integrity Framework for Public Investment[1] (OECD, 2016) proposes a set of specifically tailored measures seeking to safeguard integrity at each phase of infrastructure projects.

Key policy questions

- Are there specific measures in place in order to prevent corruption and capture from happening in infrastructure governance, such as measures to

   o prevent public officials and private sector employees from accepting or demanding bribes[2]?

   o adequately identify and manage potential and apparent conflict-of-interest situations?

   o regulate and limit the use of confidential information by public officials?

   o ensure that public investment decisions are based on national, regional or sectorial objectives?

   o prevent the selection of public investment from favouring a particular interest group/individual over the public interest?

   o ensure the objectivity and credibility of social, economic and environmental feasibility studies?

   o limit the influence of a potential private operators, construction companies or lenders?

   o ensure that the design of the tender documents and specifications are not restrictive or tailored?

   o prevent bid rigging, collusion or the agree sharing of the market or future contracts in a public investment?

- Do audit functions have adequate capacity and resources to provide timely and reliable audits, as well as to remain insulated from manipulation of audit processes?

Indicators

- Adequate conflict of interest policies for public officials (prohibitions of exercising certain activities or holding certain interests; post-employment measures; disclosure; advisory services) ;

- System of internal controls and financial reporting to monitor and identify irregularities

- Measures in place to control the integrity of firms wishing to contract with public bodies

- Mechanisms to report wrongdoing related to infrastructure projects

- Sufficient technical resources within the organisation responsible for organising public tenders

- Political contribution limits and spending limits in relation with election campaigns at national, regional and municipal levels

- Standards regulating lobbying activities and ensuring they are conducted in a transparent manner.

3. Choose how to deliver infrastructure

When choosing how to deliver an infrastructure service, i.e. delivery modality, government should balance the political, sectoral, economic, and strategic aspects. Legitimacy, affordability, risk allocation, and value for money should guide this balancing.

Definition

A delivery modality is a particular model for the delivery of infrastructure services. It can take place in a number of ways depending on the allocation of risks and the level of control retained by governments.

Why is this important?

The choice of how infrastructure is delivered and who is responsible for the project development delivery has implications for public sector discretionary control, value-for-money, risks allocation, and affordability. In many countries, however, the choice of modality is often based on habit and lacks specific criteria both for traditional infrastructure and private finance options (Burger and Hawkesworth, 2011).

One size does not fit all. There are many ways to develop infrastructure projects. Major alternatives can be found in the governance of the infrastructure and in the delivery mode. The public sector's role can vary and there are a number of hybrid forms depending the allocation of both responsibilities and risks between the public and the private sectors (See Annex C). Approaches for delivering, managing and regulating infrastructure may involve regulated privatisation, state-owned enterprises, different forms of public provision (public works, PPPs or concessions), or a combination of these. While particular infrastructure sectors typically exhibit common economic characteristics because of the nature of the assets involved and the services provided, the choice of sectoral approach (or approaches) must also take into account country (national and sub-national) circumstances. Specific projects must also be evaluated on case-by-case basis in order to identify the most appropriate delivery mode, whether public works, PPP or concession.

The OECD developed a decision tree and accompanying check lists (Annex B) that seek to raise issues that will be unique to each country and that will need to be assessed by countries in order to make specific decisions as to how infrastructure can best be delivered. Depending on risks allocation and the level of control exercised, governments can identify the most efficient delivery mode from public works to private public partnerships or a number of hybrid approaches. Assessing costs and benefits of the different option should enable countries to take a fresh look at their infrastructure delivery choices and identify where a change might add value given new priorities. For instance, if the challenge is to introduce greater cost efficiency, a greater use of market mechanisms might be beneficial, insofar as the right country circumstances are present, such as a competitive market. The framework presented offers a three-step process based on sectoral criteria, country criteria (national/sub-national levels) and project criteria. It suggests that countries:

- Identify preferred sectoral approach (or approaches) by assessing reform objectives and the characteristics of the sector

- Take into account country circumstances (political economy, government's capacities, private sector's capacities, enabling legal environment, etc.) in determining the most appropriate sectoral approach (or approaches) for a given jurisdiction

- Assess each project on a case-by-case basis to determine the most appropriate delivery mode (public works, PPP or concession).

Key policy questions:

- What are the prioritised sectoral policy objectives?

- What is the extent of market failures?

- How politically sensitive is the sector?

- What characterises the enabling public, private and legal environment?

- What is the size and financing profile of the investment?

- What is the level of control government want to retain?

- What is the potential for cost recovery?

- What is the level of uncertainty?

- Is it possible to identify, assess and allocate risk appropriately?

Indicators

- Formal set of criteria to determine project prioritisation, approval and funding

- Formal process or policy document to ensure value for money, for example by

  - Cost-benefit analysis

  - Cash flow estimates over the project cycle

  - Business case methodology

- Policy document and processes to ensure competitive tender process

- Dedicated procedure for identifying and allocating clearly risks between public and private parties

4. Ensure good regulatory design

Good regulatory design and delivery is necessary to ensure sustainable and affordable infrastructure over the life of the asset.

Definition

Regulation sets the "rules of the game" for a particular sector and market. The regulatory framework has profound impact on infrastructure investment, development, maintenance, upgrading and decommissioning. At the most basic level regulation is justified when its economic, social and environmental benefits justify the costs and net benefits are maximised. Regulation should serve the public interest and be informed by the legitimate needs of those affected by regulation. In addition to well-designed rules, good outcomes require that the implementation of these rules is overseen by regulators that enjoy adequate governance arrangements and whose mission allows for the achievement of expected economic, social, and environmental goals.

Why is this important?

Uncertainty of the "rules of the game" or their low quality will impact the willingness to invest in, maintain, upgrade and decommission infrastructure and ultimately affects the quality of service delivery. Projects often involve many policy areas, several layers of legislation and regulation, and different levels of government. For example, investment laws, public procurement laws, privatisation and concession laws, environmental protection laws, and sectoral regulations, can all affect infrastructure projects. Procedures and approval processes can be imposed at the national, sub-national, or local level. Coherence in policy, legislation and regulation, and good co-ordination between government authorities in their implementation, will simplify project development and implementation by reducing the administrative burden.

Uncertainty with regards to revenue flows (user charges/tariffs) and sources of funding (budget subsidies) through the life-cycle of the asset can result in a lack of confidence in the project's affordability from both public sector and potential investors. Setting user fees is a difficult, highly political task. Information asymmetries between governments and operators on, for instance, capital costs, asset depreciation and consumers' preferences can make tariff setting challenging. If tariffs do not cover the long-term depreciation of capital assets, for instance, investment decisions could be short-sighted and infrastructure could fail to be appropriately maintained and upgraded. Allocating subsidies from the public budget can also be a difficult process in times of fiscal stress.

A stable institutional and regulatory framework can address these challenges by creating an enabling environment for effective management of infrastructure. Regulatory institutions credibility and the trust they generate will depend on their governance, including role clarity, adequate processes and structure to manage human and financial resources, independence, accountability, performance evaluation and funding as defined in the OECD Best Practice Principles on the Governance of Regulators (OECD, 2012b).

While regulators are seldom involved in market structure decisions, they are expected to accompany and supervise the implementation of significant policy changes that affect infrastructure such as deregulation, unbundling, privatisation or tariff regulation. The information they collect and use for setting tariffs can help address information asymmetries. Regulators can bring to the table a consolidated economic or functional view of the sector or a given project, thus helping to bridge some of the co-ordination gaps that might exist between the different actors involved in the governance of infrastructure. The governance of regulators can also be taken as a reflection of the quality of the broader infrastructure investment regime. This effect can be particularly strong if the regulator is perceived as taking decisions on an objective, impartial, and consistent basis, without conflict of interest, bias or improper influence.

Key policy questions

- Is the overall regulatory framework for infrastructure sectors conducive to good governance of infrastructure?

- Are there multiple layers of regulatory requirements perceived as overly burdensome?

- Is there appropriate co-ordination between various regulatory bodies, as well as mechanisms for co-operation between regulators across borders?

- Are the functions, powers and capacities of regulators aligned with the role of regulators in the broader infrastructure permitting and approval process?

- What key data and information, including on costs of capital, asset depreciation and infrastructure consumer base, are available to inform tariff setting?

- Does the overall governance of regulators facilitate confidence and trust in the infrastructure investment regime?

Indicators

- Use of evidence-based tools for regulatory decisions

  - Impact assessment
  - Ex-post evaluation

- Regulators

  - Independence
  - Accountability
  - Sufficient scope of action

5. Integrate a consultation process

The consultation process should be proportionate to the size of the project and take account of the overall public interest and the views of the relevant stakeholders. The process should be broad-based, inspire dialogue and draw on public access to information and users' needs. Transparency is a key component of consultation process.

Definition

Consultation involves actively seeking the opinions of interested and affected groups such as business, civil society and local stakeholders, trade unions, wider interest groups, or other levels of government. It is a two-way flow of information, which may occur at any stage of infrastructure development. It may be a one-stage process or, as it is increasingly the case, a continuing dialogue.

Why is this important?

Infrastructure impacts communities - without well managed consultation good projects may falter. Consultations in democratic countries should take into account the role of elected representatives and executive to take action on behalf of the general public good in a timely fashion.

Policies, laws and large infrastructure projects should be developed in an open and transparent fashion, with appropriate and well publicised procedures for effective and timely inputs from interested local, national and (if relevant) foreign parties. Consultation processes can enhance the legitimacy of the project amongst the stakeholders[3], as well-executed consultation can bring a sense of shared ownership. Structured public consultation not only fosters ownership in infrastructure projects, it also creates opportunities for various communities to become advocates of their benefits and provide incentives for good performance (Butcher, 2014). Transparency is a key component of consultation process.

It should be noted, however, that while consultation and citizen engagement is necessary for good governance, it is not an easy undertaking. The decision maker must actively weigh views against each other in order to avoid capture by specific interests. The views of stakeholders negatively affected by infrastructure projects have to be counterbalanced by such projects' contribution to the achievement of policy outcomes for society at large. Consultations must therefore be structured in such a way that the process can be finished in a timely manner and that policy capture and other distortions are avoided.

Key policy questions [4]

- Is there an open government or consultation strategy?

- Are specific stakeholder groups consulted throughout infrastructure projects phases[5]?

- Are structured dialogue mechanisms in place to ensure systematic public consultation[6]?

- Are there formal mechanisms to involve the public in the monitoring and implementation of infrastructure investments during the construction phase and upon completion?

- Is there a forum, process or procedure for determining the balance between stakeholder interests and the public good?

Indicators

- National open government strategy or guidelines (either designed for infrastructure investments or that could be applied to them)

- Mapping of stakeholders

- Stakeholder consultation fora or participatory budgeting programmes

- Websites or other outreach tools to provide public information on infrastructure projects

- Participatory auditing procedures

6. Co-ordinate infrastructure policy across levels of government

There should be robust co-ordination mechanisms for infrastructure policy within and across levels of government. The co-ordination mechanisms should encourage a balance between a whole of government perspective and sectoral and regional views.[7]

Definition

By co-ordination across levels of government is meant procedures, institutions and other process tools that help decision-makers at different levels of government make decisions that maximise the beneficial impact of infrastructure investment and related activities throughout the country. Mechanisms used for co-ordination range from informal policy exchange platforms to formal platforms of co-ordination, to co-financing arrangements for shared responsibilities or conditionality requirements for receiving central funds (OECD, 2013).

Why is this important?

Vertical co-ordination arrangements across the national and subnational levels help reduce a series of potential gaps or contradictions between policy objectives, fiscal arrangements and regulations across levels of government, which can undermine the design and implementation of infrastructure strategies. They encourage alignment of strategic priorities and a whole of government perspective on infrastructure. Horizontal co-ordination mechanisms across jurisdictions contribute to encourage economies of scale for infrastructure investment and enhance the affordability of an asset for users.

Public investment typically involves different levels of government at some stage of the investment process - be it through shared policy competencies or joint funding arrangements. Sub-national governments (SNGs), defined as federated states, regions and municipalities, undertake almost 60% total public investment across the OECD area (OECD, 2016). A large part of this investment is spent on infrastructure. Sub-national public investment ranges from 13% in Chile to 95% in Canada.

Collaboration for public investment strategies across jurisdictions and levels of government is difficult, even in situations where the actors involved clearly recognise the need for it. Transaction costs, competitive pressures, resource constraints, differing priorities and fears that the distribution of costs or benefits from co-operation will be one-sided, can all impede efforts to bring governments together.

The national government holds a key strategic role in convening investment priorities, strengthening capacities of different levels of government involved in managing public investment, and ensuring sound framework conditions for governing public investment.

Horizontal co-operation between sub-national governments can also be important for reaching economies of scale. Though the potential benefits of co-ordination across jurisdictions may seem obvious, co-ordination was perceived as a significant challenge by most SNGs surveyed in 2015 (OECD-CoR, 2015 survey). More than three-quarters of SNGs reported the absence of a joint investment strategy with neighbouring cities or regions.

Cross-jurisdictional co-ordination can take a variety of forms, with the appropriate approach depending on the characteristics of the locality or region as well as the policy objectives and investment(s) being considered. Such co-ordination may for example take place in dialogue platforms, through the consolidation of several SNGs' plans, or through financial incentives from the national government. Horizontal cooperation may also imply the mutualisation of capital funding toward facilitating access to finance (Allain-Dupré et al, 2016).

Key policy questions

- Are the competencies related to infrastructure development allocated clearly and coherently across levels of government?

- Do financing needs match the mandates granted to subnational governments for infrastructure development?

- What are the main co-ordination challenges for infrastructure policy across levels of government?

- What are the fiscal and policy co-ordination instruments across levels of government?

- What are the governance instruments or fiscal incentives to enhance co-ordination across jurisdictions for infrastructure investment? Do they work properly?

Indicators

- Formal mechanisms/bodies for co-ordination of public investment across levels of government

- Co-ordination bodies/mechanisms have a multi-sector approach (across multiple ministries/departments)

- Co-ordination mechanisms are frequently used and produce clear outputs/outcomes

- Co-financing arrangements for infrastructure investment

- Higher levels of government provide incentives for cross-jurisdictional co-ordination

7. Guard affordability and value for money

Governments must ensure that infrastructure projects are affordable and the overall investment envelope is sustainable. The asset should represent value for money. This requires the use of dedicated processes, a capable organisation and relevant skills.

Definition

Value for money can be defined as what a government judges to be an optimal combination of quantity, quality, features and price (i.e. cost), expected over the whole of the project's lifetime. Thus, the value-for-money concept attempts to encapsulate the interests of citizens, both as taxpayers and recipients of public services. Value for money can be measured in *absolute cost-benefit terms* (do the benefits exceed the costs) or in *relative terms* (is one form of delivery more cost-effective than the other). A project and portfolio can be said to be **affordable** if the expenditure and contingent liabilities it entails for the government can be accommodated within current levels of government expenditure and revenue, including user charges, and if it can also be assumed that such levels can be sustained. An asset is affordable for users if they are willing and able to pay for it.

Why is this important?

It is the responsibility of the decision-maker to ensure public infrastructure is affordable. This requires a strong link between the project development phase and the fiscal framework of the country. A country's overall infrastructure expenditure and the fiscal risks it carries in terms of guarantees should be based on medium and long term fiscal projections and regularly updated. If the project is meant to be user funded, a careful investigation of the ability and willingness of users to pay must be conducted. Overall value for money should be carefully assessed using a combination of quantitative (such as cost/benefit analysis) and qualitative tools that soberly seek to establish the overall societal return on investment and this assessment should be evaluated by an institution different from the project leader. This process is inherently based on assumptions that are open to discussion, but as long as these are transparently treated, the process is valuable.

This process should enable decision-makers to prioritise projects so that the maximum value is generated for society as a whole. A particular issue that needs to be managed is that many politicians prefer new build projects with high visibility, rather than spending on maintaining and upgrading existing assets. This can oftentimes be a threat to value for money.

With respect to **relative value for money**, certain delivery modalities may improve the value for money compared to that realised through other forms of infrastructure delivery depending on public and private sector capabilities, the degree of certainty of future revenues and the desired allocation of risks and controls. In the face of many competing investment possibilities, the government should prioritise projects that contribute to the achievement of their development goals. Pipeline development should also be informed by the capabilities and capacities of the government itself and the potential financing market. The framework for infrastructure should not unduly favour certain types of delivery modalities due to tradition, special subsidies, accounting rules etc.

Key policy questions

- Is the infrastructure procurement process integrated into the ordinary budget process?

- Is the full cost of the asset budgeted upfront regardless of how it is implemented?

- Is there a long term infrastructure strategy and is it linked to long term fiscal projections?

- Is there a process for prioritisation across sectors and within sectors?

- Is a cost- benefit analysis carried out?

- Are various delivery modalities analysed so as to ensure value for money?

- Is an affordability analysis carried out for the public budget and/or the users?

- Are there dedicated units and capacities available to decision-makers with respect to infrastructure strategy, delivery and performance monitoring and ensuring value for money in contracting?

- Are cost-benefit analyses evaluated by an institution different from the project leader?

Indicators

- Central Budget Authority role in green-lighting infrastructure projects

- Supreme Audit Institution

- PPP or Infrastructure Unit or a procurement unit in charge of infrastructures

- Tests and controls to assess the maturity of the organisation responsible for delivering the project

- Formal requirement to account for contingent liabilities and running costs

- Formal requirement for ensuring absolute value for money

- Accounting standards

8. Generate, analyse and disclose useful data

Infrastructure policy should be based on data. Governments should put in place systems that ensure a systematic collection of relevant data and institutional responsibility for analysis, dissemination, and learning from this data. Relevant data should be disclosed to the public in an accessible format and in a timely fashion.

Definition

Relevant data would include the projected and actual performance of the asset, the cost of construction, finance, operation, the contract terms, as well as relevant procedural information.

Why is this important?

Most countries use some kind of numerical value analysis when choosing whether to pursue a particular investment as well as which delivery modality to use. The use of cost/benefit analysis, business case methodology and public sector comparators are necessarily based on assumptions as well as more verified data, including both quantitative and qualitative elements. The fundamental element that enhances the solidity of any kind of value for money test is data. Unfortunately, there is a lack of systematic data-collection regarding the cost and performance of infrastructure assets. While many countries do collect data, most of the data that would be required to compare the overall costs of projects financed through various alternative mechanisms is not systematically collected, processed or disclosed.

This lack of collection and systematic publication of data also impedes effective monitoring of assets' performance. The use of key performance indicators (KPI) to oversee the performance of infrastructure service delivery is, however, rapidly developing and proving a strong tool to monitor and benchmark the performance of infrastructure in their delivery phase. However, the experience of developing key performance indicators in the water sector for example shows the difficulty in agreeing on a common methodology for key performance indicators and the capacity needed both on the regulators' part and the utilities' part to provide meaningful quality information that inform the key processes.[8]

This lack of data collection also impedes systematic *ex post* learning, although some Supreme Audit Institutions (SAI) and some regional and local audit institutions are addressing this gap. Ideally the SAI would audit and assess individual projects, and perhaps the infrastructure programme in general, *ex post* with regards to performance, finance and compliance, but this requires dedicated resources and tools. To enhance transparency, confidence and value for money, the government should on its own disclose key data in a timely and manageable way (World Bank, 2016). This would include key budget data.

Key policy questions

- Is there a mandatory system to ensure systematic collection of relevant financial and non-financial data during the project development?

- Is there a mandatory system to ensure collection of relevant financial and non-financial data about the performance of infrastructure?

- Is there sufficient data that makes is possible to compare various forms of infrastructure delivery models? Are they compared based on data?

- Is financial and non-financial data about the project (*ex ante* and performance) disclosed to the public?

<table>
<tr><td>

Indicators

- Central unit (Central Infrastructure Unit, Central Budget Authority) for the collection, disclosure and analysis of data.

- Choice of delivery modality and projects are based on data.

- Key Performance Indicators to assess infrastructure performance

- Disclosure of data in an open format on a dedicated website

- Infrastructure investment flow data (in sectorial breakdown)

- Infrastructure investment stock data (in sectorial breakdown)

</td></tr>
</table>

9. Make sure the asset performs throughout its life

Ensure a focus on the performance of the asset throughout its lifespan by putting in place monitoring systems and institutions.

Definition

Monitoring in this context means the purposeful regular observation and recording of the performance of the asset. It is a process of systematically and routinely gathering information on all aspects relevant to the delivery of the infrastructure service to the public and users in a timely and proportional manner.

Why is this important?

It can be difficult to oversee the performance of infrastructure service delivery and hereby maintaining value for money through the performance of the asset. OECD work on the governance of water regulators (OECD, 2015b) highlights that the establishment of a regulator strengthens the public interest, makes service providers more accountable, and enables an independent price-setting process. Countries are well aware of these challenges. Some have responded by skill enhancing sectoral units, regulators, and streamlined the role and availability of specialised advisors. Others have set up dedicated units, especially in the field of PPPs, which are contract based, but increasingly with a broader remit of infrastructure in general.

The responsibility for identifying potential problems during the operational phase of the project rests primarily with the line ministry or agency. However, central agencies such as the Central Budget Authority, Supreme Audit Institution and regulatory authorities should play their part and retain the appropriate level of responsibility during the operational phase. Particular attention should be paid to contractual arrangements and monitoring capacity at later stages of a project so as to ensure that incentives do not deteriorate as the cost of noncompliance falls. Special care should also be taken to ensure that value for money is maintained during renegotiation.

Key policy questions

- Is there a strategy for how performance of the asset throughout the life of the asset is to be ensured?

- Do relevant line ministries or agencies conduct performance assessment and monitoring of each project? Are there programmes in place for training and capacitating relevant institutions?

- Do PPP/concession/procurement contracts state the required output and performance?

- Is there a strategy in case of renegotiations?

Indicators

- Policy document for ensuring performance from assets regulated by agency (sector regulator) or by contract with line department or similar.

- Clear remit of the sectorial ministries and authorities to develop, assess and monitor infrastructure policy and performance

- Strategy for re-negotiations.

- *Ex post* evaluation of value for money.

10. Public infrastructure needs to be resilient.

Infrastructure systems should be resilient, adaptable to new circumstances and future proof. Critical risks materialise and technological change can fundamentally disrupt sectors and economies.

Definition

Resilient infrastructure systems are resistant or adaptive to shock events. This quality may be achieved typically through regulatory frameworks that promote reserve capacity, diversification or back-up systems to reduce the risk of service delivery failure and/ or prolonged periods of disruption. Infrastructure operators also plan for resilience by formulating appropriate standards for business continuity and implementing them to manage risks to the operation and delivery of core services.

Why is this important?

Multiple disasters in recent years have demonstrated the significant socio-economic and environmental impacts of disasters, including internal shocks, systemic shocks, and security shocks, and the consequences for citizens who must live for an extended period without the safe drinking water and reliable electricity, communications, and mobility that infrastructure provides. Disruptions to these critical systems spread the social hardships of disasters by cutting-off access to basic life lines (health services, food, fuel, payment systems), and produce large economic impacts by preventing the mobility of labour and inventory. Examples include the Great East Japan Earthquake in 2011 caused nuclear reactors to shut down, which led to a reduction of up to 50% in power output. Hurricane Sandy flooded key roads and tunnels connecting the boroughs of Brooklyn and Manhattan as well as train, subway and electrical power lines; 5.4 million commuters were stranded without means of transportation, and power was cut to more than 8 million homes, some of which remained dark for weeks.

A governance framework that ensures resilience measures are applied to multiple critical infrastructure sectors is essential. This is due to the functional dependencies and interdependencies between different sectors of critical infrastructure. Damages to one asset, for example electricity distribution, could result in downstream disruptions to various sectors, e.g. water purification. The high share of critical infrastructure that is privately owned or operated implies the need for governments to partner with the private sector. Complementary governance approaches to regulation include those that foster regular exchanges, information sharing, mutual trust, and public cost sharing for private investment in critical infrastructure resilience.

Key policy questions

- Are there policies in place to ensure that key infrastructure assets are resilient if disasters hit?

- Are key structures designing to sustain a foreseeable shock or are substitute or redundant systems available.

- Is there management capacity to identify options, prioritising actions, and communicate decisions to the people who will implement them?

- Are there tools in place to learn from past events?

Indicators

- The presence of a disaster risk assessment plan

- The presence of designated authorities responsible for tackling disasters

---

Notes

1. www.keepeek.com/Digital-Asset-Management/oecd/governance/integrity-framework-for-public-investment_9789264251762-en#.WAhzqE1f2Uk#page1

2. See Annex Box D4 for example on training.

3. Stakeholder involvement activities can include: providing for transparent decision-making processes by making relevant information and national development plans available publicly; increasing citizen participation through public fora, participatory budgets (see Annex Box D1) and websites that allow citizens to prioritise public investments; and ensuring that relevant groups participate in the decision-making process and that groups are not inadvertently excluded (OECD, 2016).

4. More information can be found in OECD (2016), The Governance of Inclusive Growth, OECD, Paris

5. See Annex Box D2 for example.

6. See Annex Box D3 for example.

7. More information can be found in OECD (2014), *Recommendation of the OECD Council on Effective Public Investment Across Levels of Government*

8. See the experience of OFWAT in the UK in establishing KPI (in OECD (2015c), *The Governance of Water Regulators*) and the heterogeneity in KPIKPI (in OECD (2012c), *Making Water Reform Happen in Mexico*).

Bibliography

ADB 2008. Public-Private Partnership (PPP) Handbook. Asian Development Bank Institutional Document.

Amin, M. (2003), "North America's Electricity Infrastructure: Are we ready for more perfect storms?", IEEE Security and Privacy Magazine, pp. 19-25, September/October.

Australia Productivity Commission (2014), "Public Infrastructure", Productivity Commission Inquiry Report No. 71, Canberra.

Burger, P. and Hawkesworth, I. (2011), "How To Attain Value for Money: Comparing PPP and Traditional Infrastructure Public Procurement", OECD Journal on Budgeting, Volume 2011/1, OECD Publishing, Paris, http://dx.doi.org/10.1787/budget-11-5kg9zc0pvq6j

Burger, P. and Hawkesworth, I. (2011), "How To Attain Value for Money: Comparing PPP and Traditional Infrastructure Public Procurement", OECD Journal on Budgeting, Volume 2011/1, OECD Publishing, Paris, http://dx.doi.org/10.1787/budget-11-5kg9zc0pvq6j

Burger, Philippe and Ian Hawkesworth (2013), "Capital budgeting and procurement practices", OECD Journal on Budgeting, Vol. 13/1. http://dx.doi.org/10.1787/budget-13-5k3w580lh1q7

Cost Sector Transparency Initiative (2011), Transparency and accountability in the construction sector, Available at www.constructiontransparency.org/documentdownload.axd?documentresourceid=46. Last accessed 19 February 2015.

Construction Sector Transparency Initiative (2012), Press Release, www.constructiontransparency.org/documentdownload.axd?documentresourceid=8La st accessed 19 February 2015.

De Mello, L. and Sutherland, D. (2014), "Financing Infrastructure", International Centre for Public Policy, Working Paper 14-09, Andrew Young School, Georgia State University

Dobbs, R. and Pohl. H. (2013), "Infrastructure Productivity: How to Save $1 trillion a Year", McKinsey

Eberhard, A. (2007), "Matching Regulatory Design to Country Circumstances", Gridlines, Note no. 23, PPIAF, The World Bank, Washington DC.

Engel, E., Fischer. R., and Galetovic, A. (2010), "The Economics of Infrastructure Finance: Public-Private Partnerships versus Public Provision", EIB Papers: Public and private financing of infrastructure, Vol. 15, No. 1, European Investment Bank, Luxembourg

European Commission (2014), Report from the Commission to the Council and the European Parliament - EU Anti-Corruption Report, available at http://ec.europa.eu/dgs/home-affairs/e-library/documents/policies/organized-crime-and-human-trafficking/corruption/docs/acr_2014_en.pdf

Fischer, Ronald, Pablo Serra and Rodrigo Gutiérrez. (2003). "The Effects of Privatization on Firms and on Social Welfare: The Chilean Case", Latin American Research Network Working Paper R-456, Washington, DC, United States: Inter-American Development Bank, Research Department.

Flyvbjerg, B. (2014), "What You Should Know About Megaprojects and Why: An Overview", Project Management Journal, Vol. 45, No. 2, pp. 6–19, Wiley Online Library

Gordon, P. and R.G. Little (2009), "Rethinking Flood Protection: Options and Opportunities for New Orleans", Public Works Management & Policy, 14(1):37-54.

Guasch, J.L. (2004), Granting and Renegotiating Infrastructure Concessions: Doing it Right, The World Bank, Washington DC.

Hart, O. (2003). "Incomplete Contracts and Public Ownership: Remarks, and an Application to Public-Private Partnerships", The Economic Journal, Vol. 113, No 486, Royal Economic Society, Blackwell Publishing, Oxford.

Hertie School of Governance (2015), The Governance Report 2015, Oxford University Press.

HM Treasury (2013), National Infrastructure Plan 2013, December 2013

Infrastructure Australia (2013), National Infrastructure Plan, June 2013,

Little, R.G. (2004), "A Socio-Technical Systems Approach To Understanding And Enhancing The Reliability Of Interdependent Infrastructure Systems", International Journal of Emergency Management, 2(1–2):98-110.

Little, R.G. (2008), "A Clinical Approach to Infrastructure Asset Management?" in Infrastructure Reporting and Asset Management: Best Practices And Opportunities. A. Amekudzi and S. McNeil, eds. Reston, Va. The American Society of Civil Engineers.

Maier, T. and Jordan-Tank, M. (2014). Accelerating Infrastructure Delivery New Evidence from International Financial Institutions, World Economic Forum

OECD (2001), OECD Recommendation of the Council concerning Structural Separation in Regulated Industries, OECD, Paris, www.oecd.org/regreform/sectors/25315195.pdf

OECD (2002), OECD Best Practices for Budget Transparency, OECD Publishing, Paris, www.oecd.org/gov/budgeting/Best%20Practices%20Budget%20Transparency%20-%20complete%20with%20cover%20page.pdf

OECD (2005), OECD Guidelines on Corporate Governance of State-Owned Enterprises, OECD Publishing, Paris, http://dx.doi.org/10.1787/9789264009431-10-en

OECD (2007), OECD Principles for Private Sector Participation in Infrastructure, OECD Publishing, Paris, www.oecd.org/daf/inv/investment-policy/38309896.pdf

OECD (2009), Managing Water for All: An OECD Perspective on Managing Pricing and Financing, OECD Publishing, Paris, http://dx.doi.org/10.1787/9789264059498-en

OECD (2010a), Dedicated Public-Private Partnership Units: A Survey of Institutional and Governance Structures. OECD Publishing, Paris, http://dx.doi.org/10.1787/9789264064843-en

OECD (2010b), Guiding Principles on Open and Inclusive Policy Making, www.oecd.org/gov/46560128.pdf

OECD (2010c), Recommendation of the Council on Principles for Transparency and Integrity in Lobbying, OECD Publishing, Paris, www.oecd.org/gov/ethics/oecdprinciplesfortransparencyandintegrityinlobbying.htm

OECD (2011a), Making the most of public investment in a tight fiscal environment: multi-level governance lessons from the crisis, OECD publishing, Paris, http://dx.doi.org/10.1787/9789264114470-en

OECD (2011b), Meeting the Challenge of Financing Water and Sanitation, OECD Publishing, Paris, http://dx.doi.org/10.1787/9789264120525-en

OECD (2012a), Making Water Reform Happen in Mexico, OECD Publishing, Paris, http://dx.doi.org/10.1787/9789264187894-en

OECD (2012b), OECD Best Practice Principles on the Governance of Regulators, OECD Publishing, Paris, www.oecd.org/gov/regulatory-policy/governance-regulators.htm

OECD (2012c), Recommendation of the Council on Principles for Public Governance of Public-Private Partnerships, OECD Publishing, Paris, www.oecd.org/gov/oecd-recommendation-public-privatepartnerships.htm

OECD (2012d) Recommendation of the Council on Regulatory Policy and Governance, OECD Publishing, Paris, www.oecd.org/governance/regulatory-policy/2012-recommendation.htm

OECD (2013), Investing Together: Working Effectively Across Levels of Government, OECD Publishing, Paris, http://dx.doi.org/10.1787/9789264197022-en

OECD (2014a), Fostering Investment in Infrastructure: Lessons Learned from OECD Investment Policy Reviews, OECD, Paris, www.oecd.org/daf/inv/investment-policy/Fostering-Investment-in-Infrastructure.pdf

OECD (2014b), Recommendation of the Council on Digital Government Strategies, OECD Publishing, Paris. www.oecd.org/gov/digital-government/recommendation-on-digital-government-strategies.htm

OECD (2014c), Recommendation of the Council on the Governance of Critical Risks, OECD Publishing, Paris, www.oecd.org/gov/risk/recommendation-on-governance-of-critical-risks.htm

OECD (2014d), Regional Outlook, OECD Publishing, Paris, http://dx.doi.org/10.1787/9789264201415-en

OECD (2014e), The challenges and applications of cost-benefit analysis (CBA) for the preliminary feasibility study of capital investments, Government at a Glance 2015 Database, http://qdd.oecd.org/subject.aspx?Subject=17375f7e-fc6c-4a5f-81bf-5b7e6a1da53c

OECD (2014f), The Governance of Regulators, OECD Best-Practice Principles for Regulatory Policy, OECD Publishing, Paris, www.oecd.org/gov/regulatory-policy/governance-of-regulators.htm

OECD (2015a), Background note for discussion at OECD Integrity Forum: Curbing Corruption - Investing in Growth.

OECD (2015b), Governance of Water Regulators, OECD Publishing, Paris, http://dx.doi.org/10.1787/9789264231092-en

OECD (2015c), Implementation Toolkit, Effective Public Investment Across Levels of Government, www.oecd.org/effective-public-investment-toolkit/public-investment.htm

OECD (2015d), OECD Recommendation of the Council on Budgetary Governance, OECD, Paris, www.oecd.org/gov/budgeting/principles-budgetary-governance.htm

OECD (2015e), Recommendation of the Council on Public Procurement, OECD Publishing, Paris, www.oecd.org/corruption/recommendation-on-public-procurement.htm

OECD (2016), Integrity Framework for Public Investment, OECD Publishing, Paris, http://dx.doi.org/10.1787/9789264251762-en

OECD (2017), OECD Recommendation of the Council on Public Integrity, www.oecd.org/gov/ethics/recommendation-public-integrity.htm

OECD (Forthcoming), Policy Making in the Public Interest: Curbing the Risks of Policy Capture, OECD Publishing, Paris.

OECD and CoR (2015), OECD and Committee of the Regions(CoR), Results of the OECD-CoR Consultation, http://cor.europa.eu/en/documentation/brochures/Documents/Results%20of%20the%20OECD-CoR%20consultation%20of%20sub-national%20governments/2794-brochureLR.pdf

Perrow, C. (1999), Normal Accidents: Living with High-Risk Technologies, Princeton, N.J.: Princeton University Press.

Rajaram, Anand, Tuan Minh Le, Kai Kaiser, Jay-Hyung Kim, and Jonas Frank, Editors (2014). "The Power of Public Investment Management: Transforming Resources into Assets for Growth", Directions in Development, Washington, DC: World Bank

Rinaldi, S.M., Peerenboom, J.P. and T.K. Kelly (2001), "Identifying, Understanding, and Analyzing Critical Infrastructure Interdependencies," IEEE Control Systems Magazine, pp. 11-25, December.

Rosenstock, M. and Trebilcock, M. (2013), Infrastructure PPPs in the developing world: lessons from recent experience, Paper presented at the Innovation in Governance of Development Finance: Causes, Consequences and the Role of Law Conference, 9 April.

Stansbury, N. (2005), Exposing the Foundations of Corruption in Construction, in "Transparency International (Ed.) Global Corruption Report 2005, accessed on 3 April 2016 at: http://archive.transparency.org/misc/migrate/publications/gcr/gcr_2005.

Thillairajan A, Mahalingam A, Deep A (2013), Impact of private-sector involvement on access and quality of service in electricity, telecom, and water supply sectors: a systematic review of the evidence in developing countries, London: EPPI-Centre, Social Science Research Unit, Institute of Education, University of London.

U.S. Department of Homeland Security (2010), Aging Infrastructure: Issues, Research, and Technology, BIPS 01.December 2010.

U.S.-Canada Power System Outage Task Force (2004), August 14th Blackout: Causes and Recommendations.

Wells, J. (2014), "Corruption and Collusion in Construction: A view from the industry", in T. Søreide and A. Williams (Eds.) Corruption, Grabbing and Development: Real World Challenges, Cheltenham, UK and Northampton, MA, USA: Edward Elgar Publishing.

Word Bank, Data base

World Bank (2016), A framework for disclosure in Public-Private Partnerships. http://pubdocs.worldbank.org/pubdocs/publicdoc/2015/11/773541448296707678/Disclosure-in-PPPs-Framework.pdf

Zimmerman, R. (2003), "Public Infrastructure Service Flexibility for Response and Recovery in the Attacks at the World Trade Center, September 11, 2001," in Impacts of and Human Response to the September 11, 2001 Disasters: What Research Tells Us, M. F. Myers, Ed. Natural Hazards Research and Applications Information Center, University of Colorado, Boulder, CO., pp. 241-268.

Zimmerman, Rae (2009), "Understanding the Implications of Critical Infrastructure Interdependencies for Water", Published Articles and Papers, Paper 7, http://research.create.usc.edu/published_papers/7

Chapter 3

The state of play in infrastructure governance

This Chapter assesses current practices in OECD members and partners countries and links them to the different dimensions of infrastructure governance. The analysis shows that for some dimensions good practices are common among all countries, such as the use of value for money mechanisms and consultation procedure. However, many other practices recommended by the framework are less present and demand attention. Deficits can be identified, for example, with respect to long term planning, prioritisation and co-ordination practices, as well as transparent and systematic decision making. In general no single best practice country group can be identified which reflects the importance of improving infrastructure governance across countries.

Background

This Chapter presents current practices in the different dimensions of infrastructure governance among OECD members and key partners. Based on the framework of infrastructure governance previously discussed, this section draws on the results of a questionnaire[1] sent to all OECD countries and key partners to collect comparative knowledge about policies and practices of infrastructure governance and help to further develop good practice recommendations. These efforts followed the mandate from the High Level Symposium on Infrastructure Governance in February 2016 hosted by the Network of Senior Public Private Partnerships (PPP) and Infrastructure Officials at the OECD, in which the gaps in infrastructure governance and the need for data and good practices were discussed.

The analysis shows that while some "good practices" suggested by the framework can be found in a majority of the countries, others are less present and demand attention. Generally, no "best practice" country can be identified which highlights the need of better infrastructure governance across all examined countries.

The survey was conducted in the beginning of 2016 and consists of 27 responses; 25 from OECD countries, including Australia, Austria, Belgium, Chile, Czech Republic, Denmark, Estonia, Finland, France, Germany, Hungary, Ireland, Italy, Japan, Korea, Luxembourg, Mexico, New Zealand, Norway, Slovenia, Spain, Sweden, Switzerland, Turkey, and United Kingdom, and 2 non-OECD countries, namely South Africa and the Philippines. In order to avoid biased results, the survey was designed to allow countries not to answer questions and to add comments or additional answers (other). The term "respondents" refers hence not always to the entire set of 27 countries but often to a subset, that have answered the question[2]. The questionnaires were sent to the responsible line ministry (Ministry of Finance, National Treasury, Ministry of Transport or public works, among others). It needs to be noted that in Belgium and Australia regions and local authorities are mainly responsible for infrastructure investment, and the answers given refer to the Federal government only.

The institutional framework

A strong institutional framework is necessary for the delivery of the needed strategic infrastructure on time and within the budget in the long run. Central units or institution such as the Central Budget Authority, Supreme Audit Institution, PPP units and regulatory authorities should play their various roles throughout the project cycle.

Roles and responsibilities are not well defined and overlaps are common. An average of 3.1 institutions is in charge of policy guidance, ranging from one to up to eight institutions. Especially the Line Ministries (in 18 countries[3]), the Central Budget Authority (15), and the Central Infrastructure Units (13) are mainly responsible for policy guidance. Technical support is carried out by slightly less institutions, with an average of 2.5 institutions per country. It is mostly assigned to the Line Ministries (15) and the Central Infrastructure Unit (12), the two agencies that are also mainly responsible for capacity building (11 and 8, respectively). Capacity building lacks a clear assignment in many countries, with either no institution assigned or between 5 and 7 institutions being responsible. Better defined roles include audit (especially assigned to the Supreme Audit Institution) and competition control (assigned to the Competition Authority).

Line ministries are the most common institutions in charge of infrastructure governance. In 24 countries line ministries are in charge of infrastructure governance or the public procurement system. Other active institutions are Central Budget Authority (21) and Central Infrastructure Units (16). In fewer cases a Supreme Audit Institutions (15), PPP Units (12) and Competition Authorities (12) participate. Less common are Sector Regulators (10), National Public Procurement Agencies (9) and only 4 participants (Korea, South Africa, Italy and Chile) have an Independent Infrastructure Commission. Other institutions participating in infrastructure governance include regional governments, Ministries for regional development and Departments for Road Administration among others.

The line ministry is the central actor at all stages of the infrastructure governance cycle. The five stages of the infrastructure governance cycle include i) evaluation of infrastructure needs, ii) planning and structuring, iii) tendering and contracting, iv) construction, and v) operation, delivery and maintenance. Each of these relates to separate governance challenges that need to be addressed. For all stages of the infrastructure live cycle, the line ministry is the main responsible institution. Key functions attributed to the line ministry include project initiation, assessing feasibility and value for money, auditing, project approval, tender, bid evaluation, negotiation, bid approval, contact management, and payment oversight.

Overlaps of responsibilities can be identified especially for the first infrastructure cycle stages. Most overlaps can be found for evaluation and prioritisation with on average three institutions in charge, as well as preparation and structuring. Additionally to the Line Ministries, the Central Infrastructure Units are mainly responsible for evaluation and prioritisation, as well as the Central Budget Authority or Ministry of Finance, Ministry of Planning and PPP Units. Almost all functions covered by the line ministry can also be found among the PPP units as well as the Central Infrastructure Unit and the sector regulators. Construction, operation, delivery and maintenance are under the responsibilities of one or two institutions. If not under control of the Line Ministry or the Central Infrastructure Unit, these stages are controlled by other institutions, such as sector units. The Central Budget Authority has the clear functions of budgeting and project approval.

Long term strategic vision for infrastructure

Countries should establish a national long-term strategic vision that addresses infrastructure service needs, how they should be met and who is responsible for making this happen. The strategy should be politically sanctioned, co-ordinated across levels of government, take stakeholder views into account and be based on clear quantitative and qualitative assumptions.

Long term infrastructure plan

A long term national strategic vision is a politically sanctioned document that affects concrete action in terms of infrastructure services to society over the long term. This long term vision needs to address the complex and versatile issues of infrastructure, which cuts across multiple stakeholder, sectors and interest and has a long term impact on economic and social development. It should also be aligned with spatial and land-use planning policies. If applicable, strategic planning for infrastructure projects should occur through the mechanisms that exist in the spatial planning system. Special procedures designed to circumvent the spatial and land use planning system should be avoided.

Only half of the examined countries have a long term vision in form of a long term plan. About half (13) of all interviewed countries have a long term infrastructure vision in form of a strategic infrastructure plan. The remaining countries have only long term sectorial plans (11), or other forms of strategic planning, such as medium term (6-7 years) plans (Ireland) or regional plans (Philippines) (Table 3.1).

In case of an overall long term strategic infrastructure plan, the strategy is mostly anchored in central agencies with input by sub-national governments. Nine of the 13 countries with an overall long term strategy include the central government level as well as sub-national government projects above a relevant size. In Austria, Hungary, South Africa and Spain the overall long term strategy refers to the central government level only. Only in Mexico does the plan refer to the central government from a sectorial perspective, including diverse sectors[4].

Table 3.1. Does your country have an overall long term strategic infrastructure plan?

Country	Does your country have an overall long term strategic infrastructure plan?	The plan integrates both central government and sub-national government	Does your country have long-term sectorial infrastructure plans?
Australia	Yes	Yes	-
Austria	Yes	No	-
Belgium	No	-	Yes
Chile	No	-	Yes
Czech Republic	No	-	Yes
Denmark	No	-	No
Estonia	No	-	Yes
Finland	No	-	No
France	No	-	Yes
Germany	No	-	Yes
Hungary	Yes	No	Yes
Ireland	Medium term (6-7 year)	-	-
Italy	Yes	Yes	-
Japan	Yes	Yes	-
Luxembourg	No	-	No
Mexico	Yes	-	-
New Zealand	Yes	Yes	-
Norway	No	-	Yes
Republic of Korea	Yes	Yes	-
Slovenia	No	-	Yes
Spain	Yes	-	-
Sweden	Yes	Yes	-
Switzerland	No	-	Yes
Turkey	Yes	Yes	
United Kingdom	Yes	Yes	
Non-OECD			
South Africa	Yes	No	-
Philippines	Regional Plan	Yes	Yes

Note: Total respondents: 27. Other forms of strategic planning include medium term (6-7 years) (Ireland), regional plans (Philippines). (1) All responses by Australian and Belgium refer to the federal government and does not include regional and local authorities, which are mainly responsible for infrastructure investment in the two countries.

Source: OECD (2016), OECD Survey of Infrastructure Governance

Eleven of the respondents without an overall long term strategic plan have long-term sectorial infrastructure plans (Table 3.1). Most of the sectorial plans refer to transport. Other sectors include energy, health, education, and communication. Very few sectorial plans relate to integrated approaches, such as regional development as found in the Czech Republic.

Updates of these long term plans are determined by fixed time intervals. The long term impact and gestation of infrastructure requires strategic planning that is predictable and based on analysis of long term needs. However, infrastructure can be extremely sensitive to political and economic fluctuations which can impede the design and implementation of clear and coherent strategic plan. Although the update of a strategic plan is based on individual fixed time intervals (e.g. every 5 years) in 6 out of 13[5] countries, the other half base the update on either election cycles (4) or *ad hoc* political needs (2).

Key drivers of the strategic planning

Infrastructure serves multiple objectives, leading to different drivers of the strategic plan. Policy goals may include economic growth, increased productivity, affordability, inclusive development, and environmental objectives, depending on the structural, political and social conditions of the countries.

Motivations for long term strategies are heterogeneous across countries and heavily depend on the development aims and economic conditions. For the respondents with some kind of a long term strategic plan[6], several key pillars can be identified (Figure 3.1). The most common drivers are transport bottlenecks (17), regional development imbalances (14), demographical needs (12), or fiscal pressure (11), whereas social imbalances and climate change are less central.

Figure 3.1. What are the key pillars or drivers of the current strategic plan?

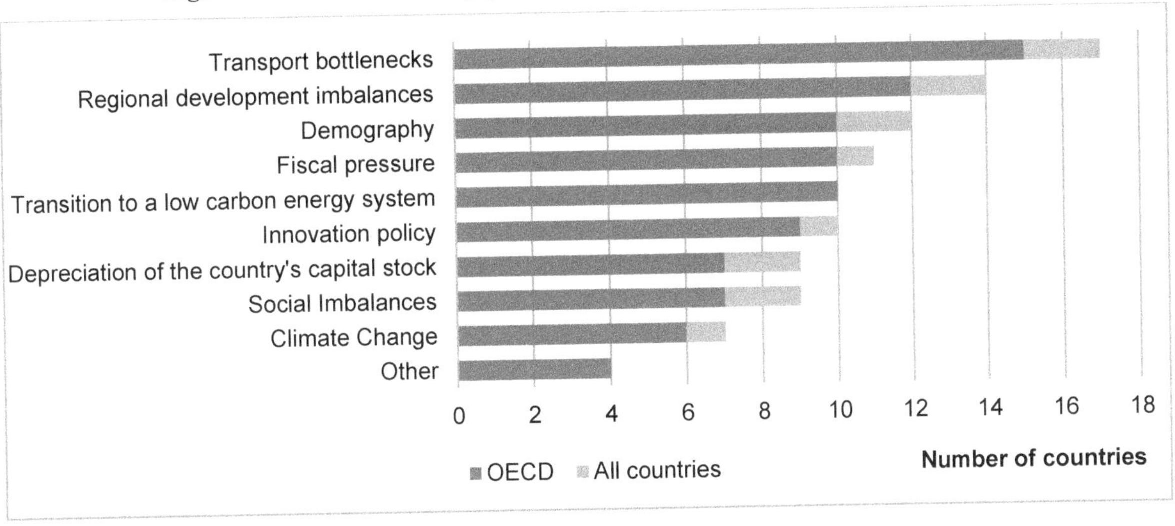

Note: Total respondents: 19. Other key drivers include specific transport goals (40% of freight traffic on rail by 2025 (Austria), a wider set of goals (Norway), determining levels of service, better asset management, optimised decision-making frameworks (New Zealand) and minimizing spatial consumption, optimizing traffic organisation in urban and semi-urban zones (Switzerland). Multiple responses allowed.

Source: OECD (2016), OECD Survey of Infrastructure Governance

Prioritisation

More than half of the respondents have a clear prioritised short list of projects. With opposing policy goals and infrastructure needs as well as time and budget constraints, a prioritisation of infrastructure projects needs to take place. In 17 of the respondents the government commits to a short list of priorities within the medium run

(Table 3.2). In case of no overall short list Norway, Germany and Czech Republic have a list of priorities at sector level in place, mainly referring to transportation[7] (waterways, railroad, and roads).

Table 3.2. Does your government have an overall short list of priority projects that it has politically committed to make happen within the medium term (e.g. an electoral cycle)?

Yes	No
Australia	Belgium
Austria	Czech Republic
Chile	Finland
Denmark	France
Estonia	Germany
Hungary	Japan
Italy[1]	Mexico
Ireland	Norway
Luxembourg	Spain
New Zealand	Sweden
Korea	
Slovenia	
Switzerland	
Turkey	
United Kingdom	
Non-OECD	
Philippines	
South Africa	

Note: Total respondents: 27; (1) According to the Infrastructure Attachment to the DEF (Document of Economy and Finance) approved in 2015, Italy has a short list of 25 priority projects, which is currently under discussion and will be replaced by a new multi-year planning document.

Source: OECD (2016), OECD Survey of Infrastructure Governance

Results from a cost-benefit analysis are the strongest argument for projects making it into the short list. Instead of an explicit value threshold, the most important element for projects that get on the short list are strong results of the cost-benefit analysis, followed by strong political backing, and the project's part of the long term strategic plan (Figure 3.2). Other important criteria include the project's functional fit with other infrastructure assets and its importance for the development of a particular sector. Less important are the private sector's interests, market failures, and strong popular backing. External funding from the EU or other donors is the least important. These results confirm the finding of the OECD (2014) study on challenges and applications of cost-benefit analysis, stating that cost benefit analysis is an important but not exclusive tool in preliminary feasibility study of capital investments.

Figure 3.2. What criteria determine whether a project gets on the short list of priority projects?

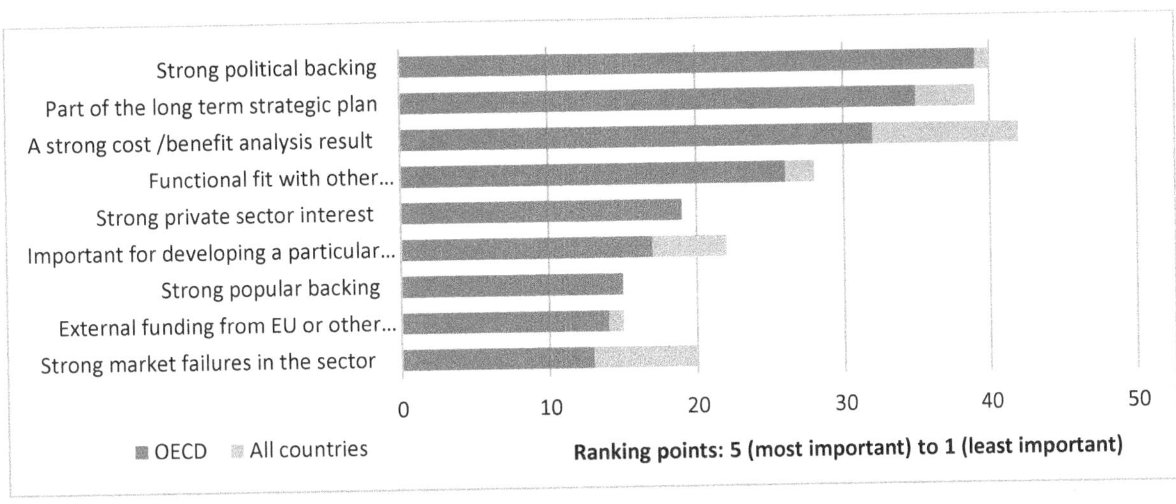

Note: Total respondents: 16 (Countries with an overall shortlist of priority projects); the criteria for the determination of the short list projects could be rated by one to five points. The ranking is based on the final sum of all rating point assigned to the criteria.

Source: OECD (2016), OECD Survey of Infrastructure Governance

The project's rank *within* the shortlist is often based on political considerations (Table 3.3). Once the project is on the short list, the political agenda is considered the most important criteria for the project's rank by 8 countries, followed by relative value for money (3) and cost-benefit (3). Estonia and the UK use a combination of criteria and Australia does not rank its priority projects. They are divided into high priority and low priority, based on to what extent the projects address national needs.

Table 3.3. Within the short list, what determines a project's rank?

Cost-benefit analysis	Political interest/agenda	Relative value for money	Combination	Other
Korea	Chile	Austria	United Kingdom	Australia[1]
New Zealand	Denmark	Slovenia	Estonia	
Non-OECD	Hungary			
South Africa	Italy			
	Ireland	**Non-OECD**		
	Luxembourg	Philippines		
	Turkey			
	Switzerland			

Note: Total respondents: 17 (Countries with an overall shortlist of priority projects); (1) Note: Australia does not rank its priority projects, but are divided into high priority and low priority, based on to what extent the projects address national needs.

Source: OECD (2016), OECD Survey of Infrastructure Governance

Integration of infrastructure planning with general spatial planning

Spatial planning processes intend to co-ordinate the spatially relevant dimensions of many public policies. They aim at obtaining efficient patterns of development and to prevent and mediate conflicts over land uses. By its nature, infrastructure development is a key element of the spatial planning process. Infrastructure is specific to particular locations and has therefore important consequences on aspects such as the distribution of economic activity across space, the spatial distribution of population and land use patterns. The feasibility of many infrastructure projects depends on existing land use patterns, while at the same time infrastructure exerts considerable influence on the future land use patterns.

Due to the importance of infrastructure for spatial outcomes strategic infrastructure planning should be integrated in the general spatial planning process. If strategic infrastructure planning processes exist that are independent from general spatial planning processes they need to be closely co-ordinated with each other. Importantly, such co-ordination should not only ensure that no immediate conflicts between the different plans exist (for example, because they assign conflicting land uses to particular areas). It should also ensure that the strategic elements of the plans, such as overarching policy objectives and fundamental strategies to achieve them, are aligned with each other.

In practical terms, the reasons for the need for co-ordination are twofold. First, there is an obvious need to co-ordinate infrastructure planning with other planning to maximise the return on infrastructure. Transport-oriented development is an example. To use transport infrastructure efficiently, land should be developed at particularly high densities around transport hubs, which requires the co-ordination of transport and land use planning.

Second, integration of infrastructure planning in the spatial and land use planning framework can help to reduce the costs of constructing infrastructure. Once land is developed, it is expensive and politically difficult to build infrastructure on it. Frequently, it requires expropriations and costly compensations. Thus, it is preferable to project infrastructure needs into the future and develop land in a way that is compatible with them (or protect land from development entirely to reserve it for future infrastructure). To do this effectively, close co-ordination of strategic infrastructure planning with land-use planning is required.

The central role of institutions

The importance of infrastructure policy is reflected by there being institutions devoted to it. In 19 countries, official institutions are officially charged with developing, assessing and monitoring infrastructure policy and performance (Table 3.4). Most of the named institutions operate on national level. Only 9[8] out of 45[9] listed institutions are situated on subnational level.

Table 3.4. Are there official institutions charged explicitly with developing, assessing and monitoring infrastructure policy and performance?

Yes	No
Australia	Austria
Chile	Belgium
Denmark	Czech Republic
Estonia	Finland
France	Hungary
Germany	Luxembourg
Ireland	Slovenia
Italy	Switzerland
Japan	
Mexico	
New Zealand	
Norway	
Korea	
Spain	
Sweden	
Turkey	
United Kingdom	
Non-OECD	
Philippines	
South Africa	

Note: Total respondents: 27

Source: OECD (2016), OECD Survey of Infrastructure Governance

Most institutions are responsible for the development of infrastructure policy and the improvement of infrastructure performance. For infrastructure policy the development of the policy is the most prevalent remit (22 institutions in 12 countries) (Figure 3.3). Another important task is the assessment of infrastructure policies (8). For the performance of infrastructure assets, 14 institutions have their remit in improvement of performance of the infrastructure asset. Fewer institutions have their remit in the assessment of performance (8) or monitoring (6). Furthermore, institutions are charged with tasks such as research and advice, cost approval and budgeting, encouraging best practices, implementation and maintenance. If there is no central official institution charged explicitly with developing, assessing and monitoring infrastructure policy and performance, these tasks are part of the sectorial ministries and authorities, such as the new Norwegian Railway Directorate, effective from 1 January 2017. This reflects previously identified tendency for overlaps in early stages, in contrast to a lack of dedicated institutions towards the end of the project cycle.

Figure 3.3. What is the remit of central infrastructure institutions (number of institutions)?

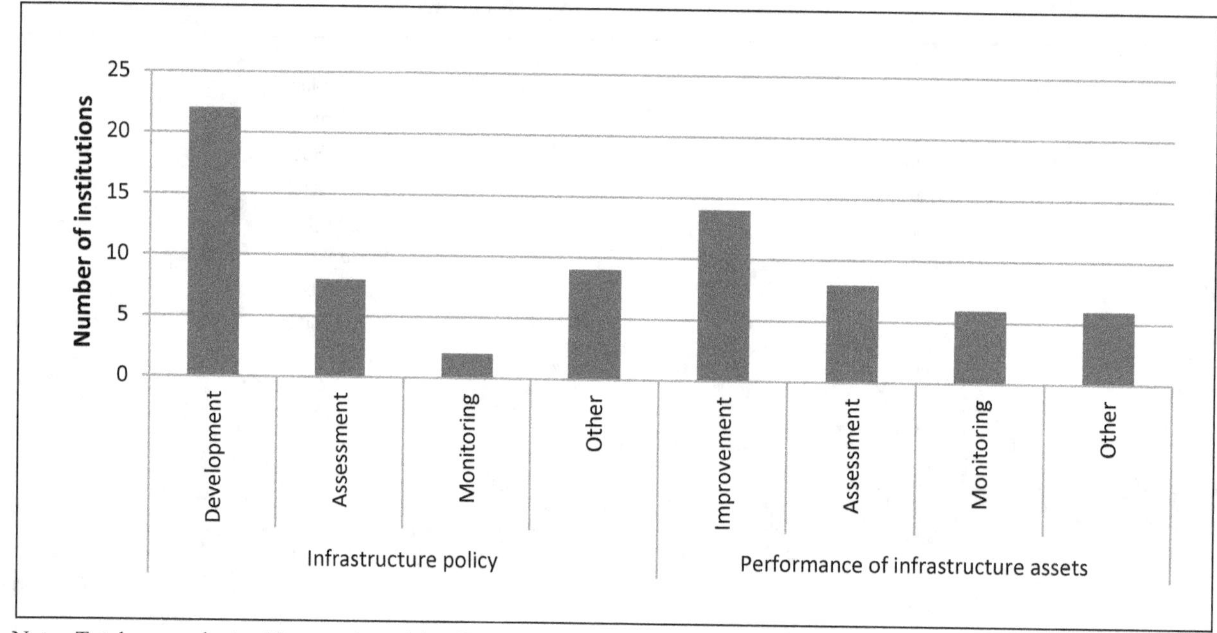

Note: Total respondents: 18 countries with official institutions charged explicitly with developing, assessing or monitoring infrastructure policy and performance, listing up to 4 institutions per country.
Source: OECD (2016), OECD Survey of Infrastructure Governance

Threats to integrity

Opportunities to derive illicit rents should be mitigated at each stage of the development of public infrastructure projects. As many actors in the public and private sectors can be vulnerable to integrity risk in infrastructure projects, a whole of government approach is essential to effectively address these risks.

The OECD Integrity Framework for Public Investment (2016) and the OECD Framework on Infrastructure Governance highlight the high vulnerability of infrastructure projects to corruption and rent seeking. The scale and complex nature of infrastructure projects, the various opportunities for public officials to exercise discretion, the numerous stakeholders involved and multiple stages of development bear integrity risks at all stages of the infrastructure investment and governance cycle. Added-value for the local or national economy, fiscal prudence, cost-effectiveness and resilience of infrastructure may be severely undermined when infrastructure projects are meant to unduly benefit inefficient economic actors and organised crime, or to disproportionately benefit political parties' or candidates' donors or core electoral base at the expense of society as a whole.

Half of examined countries applied specific measures against corruption in infrastructure. For 15 of the respondents (Table 3.5), a specific anti-corruption law is in place. Twelve of those countries find that these measures have achieved their intended impact. Measures implemented by the countries surveyed to prevent corruption in infrastructure projects include making private firms subject to spot checks by external auditors, codes of conduct for private contractors, and online warning systems to share discovered corruption schemes or warning signs among relevant agencies on a real time basis.

Table 3.5. Is there a specific law in place that seeks to minimise the risk of corruption in infrastructure governance (additional to a generic anti-corruption law)?

Is there a specific law in place?	Has the law generally the intended impact
Belgium	Belgium
Czech Republic	Czech Republic
Denmark	Denmark
France	France
Germany	Germany
Ireland	Ireland
Luxembourg	Luxembourg
Mexico	Norway
Norway	Philippines
Korea	Korea
Slovenia	Spain
Spain	Turkey
Turkey	
Non-OECD	
Philippines	
South Africa	

Note: Total respondents: 27

Source: OECD (2016), OECD Survey of Infrastructure Governance

A majority (21) of all respondents have an explicit policy in place that regulates conflicts of interest in the tender panel. The numerous and diversified actors involved in the infrastructure governance process produce conflicts of interests in the tender panel. Furthermore, opaqueness, corruption and favouritism are often associated with the tendering phase, despite the fact that these may be present in other phases of the infrastructure development cycle. Policy guidelines, laws and regulations are necessary to avoid conflict of interest at all phases of infrastructure projects, which may impede optimal outcomes. In 15 countries, conflicts of interests are subject to an explicit policy that takes the form of a law or regulation, whereas others give policy guidelines.

Of the total respondents, 17 countries have implemented a remedies system and 22 countries provide for appeal mechanisms in the tendering process. Remedies systems, which are procedures, such as cancellation of the delivery process or compensation, by which an excluded bidder can contest the decision to award the contract to another supplier, are in place in 17 countries. Appeal mechanisms, which provide an opportunity to challenge initial decisions, are present in 22 countries. Decisions can usually be challenged on the basis of alleged violation of the law or general procurement principles, such as fairness, transparency, equal treatment, among others. These measures are important to ensure integrity and fairness in tendering (Figure 3.4).

**Figure 3.4. Please, indicate whether the measures listed below
are in place in your country**

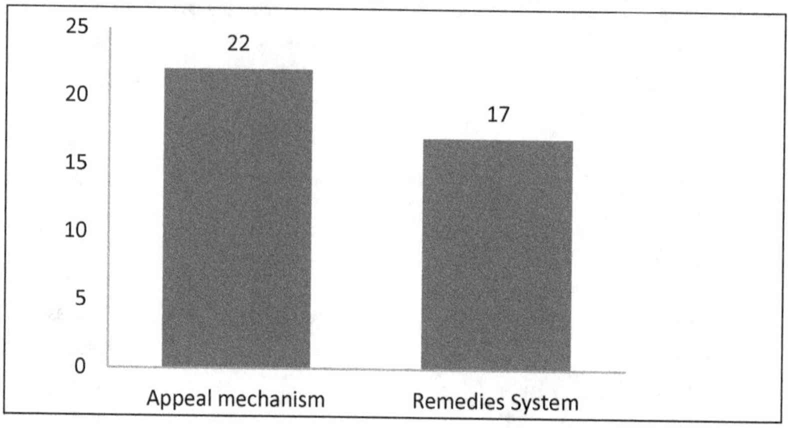

Note: Total respondents: Appeal mechanism: 24; Remedies System: 20 (countries without mechanisms are not displayed)

Source: OECD (2016), OECD Survey of Infrastructure Governance

Infrastructure procurement and the choice of the delivery modality

The choice of the delivery modality should balance political, sectoral, economic, and strategic aspects.

Instead of applying one method to all projects by default, countries should determine the delivery mode or portfolio of projects by the relevant national, sectorial, and project characteristics. The Framework for the Governance of Infrastructure offers a set of criteria for assessing an appropriate delivery modality, including project size and profile, revenues and usage, the level of uncertainty and risk allocation (Annex B, Box B1).

The most relevant criteria determining the delivery modality are financial criteria. The most important criteria for the determination of the delivery modality include for example the availability of public sector financial resources, availability of public sector capacity of handling the project, the wish to tab private finance sources to augment the pubic budget, the degree to which cost recovery possible from users, as well as the outcome of a quantitative analysis. Additional to financial criteria individual country needs make specific procurement or delivery modes more likely (Table 3.6).

Table 3.6. Most important criteria that make the listed methods more likely?

Delivery mode: **Public works**	**PPP/concessions**	**Regulated private assets**	**State owned enterprises (SOE)**
Is there public sector capacity of handling these kinds of projects	Is there private sector capacity of handling these kinds of projects	The wish to use private finance sources to augment the pubic budget	Political sensitivity to private sector participation
Tradition in the sector for a certain delivery modality	The need for sharing risks with private actors	Is there private sector capacity of handling these kinds of projects	The degree to which cost recovery is possible from the user
Availability of public sector financial resources	The outcome of a quantitative comparison (relative value for money test) between traditional public works or other forms of private sector participation	The need for sharing risks with private actors	Is there public sector capacity of handling these kinds of projects

Table 3.6. Most important criteria that make the listed methods more likely? *(cont.)*

Delivery mode: **Public works**	**PPP/concessions**	**Regulated private assets**	**State owned enterprises (SOE)**
Extent of government control	The wish to use private finance sources to augment the pubic budget	The need for building up a market for alternative ways of procuring public infrastructure (e.g. PPPs)	Strength of business case
Political sensitivity to private sector participation	The need for building up a market for alternative ways of procuring public infrastructure (e.g. PPPs)	The degree to which cost recovery is possible from the user	Tradition in the sector for a certain delivery modality

Note: Total respondents: 27

Source: OECD (2016), OECD Survey of Infrastructure Governance

A number of criteria point to a private finance delivery, such as PPPs or concessions. The most influential criteria is the outcome of a quantitative comparison (relative value for money test) between traditional public works and other forms of private sector participation, the need for increased innovation, the need for sharing risks with the private sector, the need for building up a market for alternative ways of procuring public infrastructure (e.g. PPPs), and the capacity of the private sector to handle these kinds of projects. The wish to use private finance sources to augment the pubic budget and the degree to which cost recovery is possible from the user as well as the wish to tap private finance sources to augment the public budget are also of high importance.

Criteria that favour the use of public works focus on capacity and habit. The likeliness of public works depends especially on the capacity of the public sector capacity of handling these kinds of projects, the tradition in the sector for a certain delivery modality, the availability of public sector financial resources and the extent of government control.

Political sensitivity to private sector participation and the degree, to which cost recovery is possible from the user, are the criteria that influence most the decision for SOEs. Few of the listed criteria are considered as enhancing the likelihood of regulated private assets.

Although prioritisation and long term planning should help to separate the decision of new infrastructure assets from the delivery methods, less than the half of the respondents do so (Table 3.7). The decision to invest in new infrastructure assets is separate in 10 countries, whereas it is combined in 13 countries. These results are similar to OECD findings (Hawkesworth and Burger, 2011), that in 11[10] countries the government first decide on the procurement of an asset before it chooses the mode of delivery.

Table 3.7. Is the decision to invest in a new infrastructure asset separate from how to procure and finance the project?

Yes	No
Australia	Austria
Denmark	Belgium
Germany	Chile
Ireland	Czech Republic
Italy	Estonia
Luxembourg	Finland
Norway	France
Turkey	Hungary
United Kingdom	Mexico
	Korea
	Slovenia
	Spain
	Sweden
	Switzerland
	Japan[na]
Non-OECD	**Non-OECD**
Philippines	South Africa[na]

Note: Total respondents: 25, In New Zealand business cases consider the strategic, economic, commercial, financial and management components, [na] not answered

Source: OECD (2016), OECD Survey of Infrastructure Governance

Good regulatory design and delivery

Good regulatory design and delivery promotes sustainable and affordable infrastructure over the entire life of the asset.

The regulatory framework has profound impact on infrastructure investment, across all levels of the infrastructure life-cycle. Nevertheless, even if well designed, good outcomes require an adequate implementation of these rules and standards that are aligned with the economic, social and environmental goals set by the policy makers.

The overall regulatory framework provides formal processes for good infrastructure governance in most countries, which are perceived as effective. A majority of the countries (14) found that the infrastructure regulation in their countries is fulfilling its role (Table 3.8). Among challenges to effective regulation are the lack of standardised evaluation criteria, the changing use of infrastructure, technical innovation, lacking capacities and skills, as well as cost and time pressure. Other widespread regulations of the infrastructure governance process are policies ensuring competitive tendering, processes regulating the tender panel, policies for allocating sufficient resources and monitoring capacity ensuring value for money in contracting, formal policies ensuring performance assessment of each project by the relevant line ministry or agency, and explicit policies that seek to minimize the risk of corruption in infrastructure governance.

Table 3.8. In general, is the infrastructure regulation fulfilling its intended role?

Yes	To some extent
Australia	France
Belgium	Ireland
Czech Republic	South Africa
Denmark	Turkey
Finland	
Germany	
Hungary	
Italy	
Japan	
Korea	
New Zealand	
Norway	
Philippines	
Switzerland	
United Kingdom	

Note: *Total respondents: 27*
Source: OECD (2016), OECD Survey of Infrastructure Governance

Functions, powers and capacities of regulators are often unclear and co-ordination is lacking. As discussed in the beginning of this chapter, a strong institutional framework with a clear distribution of responsibilities is necessary for the efficient delivery of strategic infrastructure. In most cases the line ministries are the most common institutions in charge of infrastructure governance throughout all stages of the infrastructure governance cycle. However, several countries[11] stated that co-ordination was weak and special dedicated bodies were missing, as well as sufficient check points for oversight institutions along the project cycle.

The lack of systematic data collection impedes the use of evidence-based tools for regulatory decisions. Nineteen of the respondents have no central, systematic and formal collection of information on financial and non-financial performance of the infrastructure projects (see *Section on Generation, Analysis and Disclosure of Data* for more information). This however is elementary to base future regulatory decision, as for example the decision of the modality of infrastructure delivery.

A more comprehensive analysis of the role of infrastructure regulators that investigates the current challenges of infrastructure regulation and the resulting implications for infrastructure governance is underway by the OECD's Network of Economic Regulators.

Consultation

The process for managing infrastructure should rest on broad-based consultations and open dialogue drawing on public access to information and a focus on users' needs. Public consultation processes are essential for legitimacy, transparency and the identification of infrastructure needs and can thus enhance the performance of infrastructure projects.

Mandatory consultation processes are used at all stages of the infrastructure governance process across the countries. In 20 countries there are mandatory consultancy processes (Table 3.9), which mainly take places during the infrastructure project preparation phase (Figure 3.5). In more than half of the countries, consultation is also mandatory for the evaluation of infrastructural needs and for the decision process of prioritising infrastructure projects. During the construction phase, mandatory consultation is less common. The feedback of these consultation processes are for example used for environmental impact studies (decision and prioritisation of infrastructure), to incorporate results from public hearings into the infrastructure preparation period, as well as analysis and evaluation throughout the project.

Table 3.9. Are there mandatory consultation processes that regulate engagement between the public, other stakeholders and the authorities during the development of a particular infrastructure project?

Yes	No
Australia	Belgium
Austria	Finland
Chile	Luxembourg
Czech Republic	Mexico
Denmark	Turkey
Estonia	Japan[na]
France	
Germany	
Hungary	
Ireland	
Italy	
New Zealand	
Norway	
Korea	
Slovenia	
Spain	
Sweden	
Switzerland	
United Kingdom	
Non-OECD	**Non-OECD**
Philippines	South Africa

Note: Total respondents: 26, [na] not answered

Source: OECD (2016), OECD Survey of Infrastructure Governance

Figure 3.5. At which stages of development do consultation processes take place?

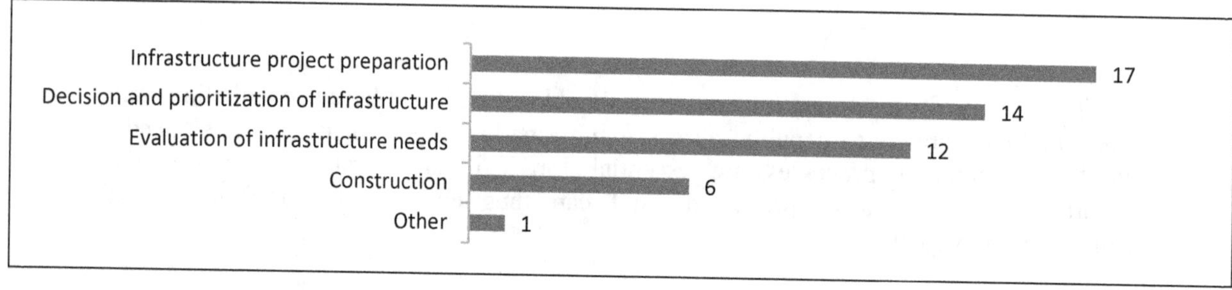

Note: Total respondents: 21 (Countries with mandatory consultation processes), (Others: not specified)

Source: OECD (2016), OECD Survey of Infrastructure Governance

A procedure to specifically identify users' needs is only mandatory in 13 countries (Table 3.10). Consultation is a strong opportunity for various stakeholders to communicate their needs and concerns. Although consultancy processes are in place in most of the examined countries, less than half have mandatory procedures for identifying and incorporating user needs. Reported procedures include consultations of the local community and the civil society (public hearings), or environmental protection issues. Italy only recently introduced a mandatory system by the adoption of the new Code of Contracts (April 2016) and the introduction of Public Debate as mandatory consultation process prior to the project development of strategic infrastructures.

Table 3.10. Is there a mandatory procedure for identifying and incorporating user needs specifically?

Yes	No
Australia[1]	Austria
Chile	Belgium
Denmark	Czech Republic
Germany	Estonia
Italy	Finland
Hungary	France
New Zealand	Luxembourg
Norway	Mexico
Korea	Spain
Slovenia	Turkey
Sweden	Switzerland
United Kingdom	Ireland[na]
	Japan[na]
Non-OECD	**Non-OECD**
South Africa	Philippines

Note: Total respondents: 25, [na] not answered; (1) There is no mandatory process, but consultation is widely considered. Most planning and consultation responsibilities are carried out by state and territory authorities.

Source: OECD (2016), OECD Survey of Infrastructure Governance

It is widespread to have a public consultation regarding the long-term strategic plan. Out of the 13 countries with long term strategies, 11 countries have consultation processes (Table 3.11). The public consultation process described is a hearing among stakeholders such as user groups, the civil society or lower levels of government.

Table 3.11. Is there a public consultation process regarding the long-term strategic plan?

Yes	No
Australia	Austria
Hungary	Italy
Japan	
Mexico	
New Zealand	
Korea	
Spain	
Sweden	
Turkey	
United Kingdom	
Non-OECD	
South Africa	

Note: Total respondents: 13 (Countries with a long-term strategic plan)
Source: OECD (2016), OECD Survey of Infrastructure Governance

Co-ordination across levels of governments

Since a large part of infrastructure investment is conducted at the subnational level, there should be robust co-ordination mechanisms for infrastructure policy within and across levels of government.

If there is a long term strategic plan, it is co-ordinated across levels of governments. In Australia, Italy, Japan, New Zealand[12], Korea, Sweden, Turkey, and the United Kingdom the strategic plans include both central government as well as sub-national government projects above a relevant size. This represents with 8 out of 13 the majority of countries that have long term strategic plans.

In total, 15 of the respondents have intergovernmental co-ordination mechanisms for infrastructure in place. These include 8 standing committees and 4 secretariats. In 8 out of these cases, these co-ordination committees are mandatory for all relevant bodies. The listed intergovernmental co-ordination include regional development councils, bilateral working groups, the International Transport Forum (OECD), EU-Council, EU-TEN and the G7 meeting of transport ministers.

Few central units aim to strengthen the capacities of sub-national governments. Only in 10 out of 27 countries national PPP units or Infrastructure Units in the Central Government have the mandate to strengthen the capacities of sub-national governments for PPPs and general infrastructure projects, but 3 do so without the mandate (Table 3.12).

Table 3.12. Do national PPP units or Infrastructure Units in the Central Government strengthen the capacities of sub-national governments (municipalities, regions, states) to design and run PPP or infrastructure projects in general?

Yes	No
Australia	Austria
Czech Republic*	Belgium
France	Chile
Germany	Denmark
Ireland*	Estonia
Italy	Finland
Korea	Hungary
Spain	Japan
Turkey*	Luxembourg
United Kingdom	New Zealand
	Norway
	Slovenia
	Sweden
Non-OECD	Switzerland
Philippines	Mexico[na]
South Africa	

Note: Total respondents: 26; * without a mandate, [na] not answered

Source: OECD (2016), OECD Survey of Infrastructure Governance

Affordability and value for money

Governments must ensure that infrastructure projects are affordable and the overall investment envelope is sustainable. Infrastructure life-cycle costs should represent value for money. This requires the use of dedicated processes, a capable organisation and the availability of relevant skills.

The most common criterion to assess a project's relative affordability is a quantitative comparison. A majority of the countries have a process to carry out a quantitative comparison between different delivery methods, either in all cases (5), all cases above a certain threshold (7) or on an ad hoc basis (11) or only for PPP projects (Mexico) (Table 3.13).

Table 3.13. Is there a process to carry out a quantitative comparison between different delivery modes?

Yes in all cases	No	Only PPP Projects	On an ad hoc basis	In all cases above a certain threshold
Germany	Austria	Mexico	Czech Republic	Australia
Norway	Chile		Belgium	France
Spain	Japan[na]		Denmark	Ireland
Italy			Estonia	Korea
			Finland	Slovenia
			Hungary	
			Luxembourg	Turkey
			New Zealand	
			Sweden	
Non-OECD			Switzerland	**Non-OECD**
Philippines			United Kingdom	South Africa

Note: Total respondents: 26, [na] not answered; (1) since the approval of the Guidelines for ex ante public investments assessment in November 2016.

Source: OECD (2016), OECD Survey of Infrastructure Governance

> ### Box 3.1. Value For Money (VfM)
>
> **"Value for money"** can be defined as what a government judges to be an optimal combination of quantity, quality, features and price (i.e. cost), expected over the whole of the project's lifetime". It can be measured in absolute cost benefit terms or in relative terms in comparison to other delivery modalities. Value for money is essential for ensuring affordability and sustainability and helps policy makers to prioritise projects so that the maximum value is generated for society as a whole. In contrast to a quantitative analysis, it combines quantitative and qualitative tools to estimate the overall societal return on an investment. Therefore value for money should be ensured by a formal process or legal regulations.
>
> *Source*: OECD, 2015

There is a formal process for ensuring absolute value for money takes place in the majority of the case (Table 3.14). However, only 5 respondents apply a value for money (Box 3.1) test for all projects[13], while 9 countries use them for projects above a certain value, others on ad hoc basis (5) or only for PPPs (Mexico).

Table 3.14. Is there a formal process/legal requirement for ensuring absolute value for money from infrastructure projects?

Yes in all cases	In all cases above a certain value threshold	No	Only PPP Projects	On an *ad hoc* basis
Australia[1]	Hungary	Austria	Mexico	Belgium
Germany	Ireland	Chile		Czech Republic
France[1]	Japan	Estonia		Denmark
Italy	New Zealand	Luxembourg		Finland
United Kingdom	Norway	Slovenia		Switzerland
	Korea	Spain		
	Turkey	Sweden		
	Non-OECD			
	Philippines			
	South Africa			

Note: Total respondents: 27; (1) Eiter by Infrastructrure Australia or the budget department; 2). excluding projects financed by local authorities

Source: OECD (2016), OECD Survey of Infrastructure Governance

Cost-benefit analysis is the most popular approach to determine absolute value for money (Figure 3.6). Used by 21 of all respondents, cost-benefit analysis including Total Cost of Ownership (TOC) during the life-cycle is the most popular approach, followed by cash-flow estimates over the project cycle (17). About 13 respondents use business case methodology. The popularity of cost-benefit studies is also found in a 2014 OECD (2014) survey of cost-benefit analysis for capital investments (Box 3.2).

Figure 3.6. What approaches are used for determining value for money?

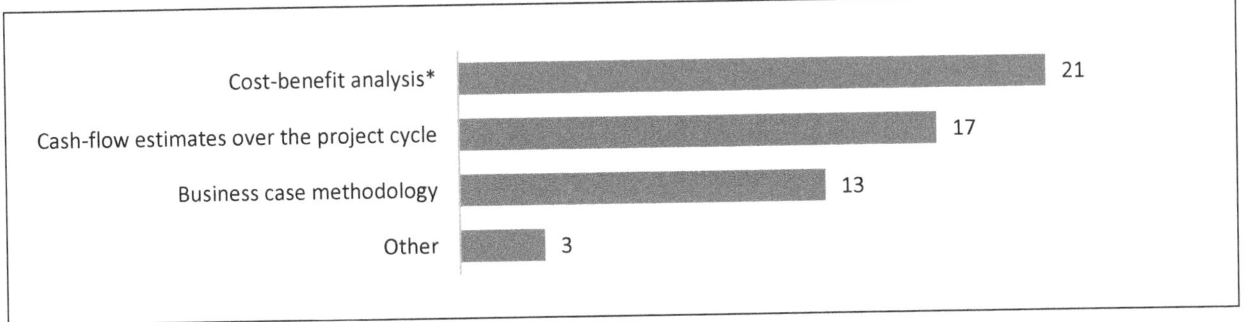

Note: Total respondents: 26, * including TCO during the life-cycle
Source: OECD (2016), OECD Survey of Infrastructure Governance

Methods mostly do not differ between sectors. Only for 7[14] countries methods differ with regards to different aspects. For example, in the Philippines social projects consider shadow pricing; in New Zealand discount rates may vary between sectors; whereas in South Africa cost benefit analysis is used in economic infrastructure, and cost effectiveness analysis for social projects.

Box 3.2. OECD (2014) survey results on challenges and applications of cost-benefit analysis for the preliminary feasibility study of capital investments

The purpose of this short survey, conducted in November 2014 including 20 OECD countries, was to identify and analyse practices in cost-benefit analysis (CBA), and to assess challenges and potential solutions to its application in OECD member countries. The main findings of survey include:

(i) *A clear finding is that CBA is an important tool for decision-making in all the surveyed member states.* Nevertheless, CBA is not considered to be able to stand alone but should complement other types of assessment, such as environmental impact assessment. The most important role is to provide justification for project selection and financing. For about half of the respondents it is furthermore considered as an accounting, transparency and monitoring tool. In most countries CBA is prepared in the pre-feasibility stage when several project alternatives should be assessed (11) or in the feasibility phase, when the prefer project alternative is already chosen (7). Few countries conducted CBA regularly after the completion of the project.

(ii) *Generally, there are legal requirements for CBA either on national, regional, or local level.* Out of 20 respondents 17 have mandatory legislation to perform CBA in place, either nationwide for all capital investment projects above a certain financial threshold (8), for specific categories of projects (1), or on state, regional or local basis (8). For few countries (8) there are specific legal requirements in terms of what the CBA should contain.

(iii) *The most systematic use of CBA is found for transport, but in several countries additional sectors are covered.* CBA is initially developed for transport infrastructures but is extended to become a general and flexible framework that is applied to other sectors. More than half of the examined countries apply CBA to the sectors of water, energy, environment, health, education, information and communication technology (ICT) and scientific research. Less usage of CBA is documented in culture and technological development and innovation.

(iv) *In several countries there is no central co-ordinating body for CBA.* Multiple government bodies, such as line ministries, agencies, and decentralised sub-national levels of governments apply their own CBA practices, leading to lacking consistency and co-ordination. Only few countries consider CBA as a strategic planning tool for prioritising investment at the central level. Some attempts of governments to meet this need of co-ordination are reflected in guidelines and supporting documents, which however, according to the survey is mostly done sector by sector rather than by a central body. For several countries however (12), there are values of key parameters and unit values set by central government bodies or by sub-national levels to use for costs and benefits.

> ### Box 3.2. OECD (2014) survey results on challenges and applications of cost-benefit analysis for the preliminary feasibility study of capital investments *(cont.)*
>
> (iv) *In several countries there is no central co-ordinating body for CBA.* Multiple government bodies, such as line ministries, agencies, and decentralised sub-national levels of governments apply their own CBA practices, leading to lacking consistency and co-ordination. Only few countries consider CBA as a strategic planning tool for prioritising investment at the central level. Some attempts of governments to meet this need of co-ordination are reflected in guidelines and supporting documents, which however, according to the survey is mostly done sector by sector rather than by a central body. For several countries however (12), there are values of key parameters and unit values set by central government bodies or by sub-national levels to use for costs and benefits.
>
> (v) *Disclosure of CBA to the public is limited.* Only a third of the examined countries (7) make the CAB of major capital investments publically available and used CBA analysis to inform public consultation and debate.
>
> *Source:* OECD (2014), The challenges and applications of cost-benefit analysis (CBA) for the preliminary feasibility study of capital investments, Government at a Glance 2015 Database, http://qdd.oecd.org/subject.aspx?Subject=17375f7e-fc6c-4a5f-81bf-5b7e6a1da53c

Affordability is an important factor when it comes to the decision whether and how an infrastructure project will be delivered. An infrastructure project can be said to be affordable if the expenditure and contingent liabilities it entails for the government can be accommodated within current levels of government expenditure and revenue, including user charges, and if it can also be assumed that such levels can be sustained.

Almost all respondents have some kind of assessment of affordability for the public budget in place *(*Table 3.15*)*: In 13 cases all projects have to be assessed, 8 countries only assess projects above a threshold, and 3 countries assess certain projects only. An assessment for users (Table 3.16) is in place for all projects in 7 of the cases, for all projects above a threshold for 4, for certain projects in 7 cases. Responsible institutions for the assessment are in many cases the Ministry of Finance or the corresponding line ministry.

Table 3.15. Are projects subject to an assessment of their affordability for the public budget?

All projects	All projects above a threshold	Certain projects	None
Belgium	Austria	Chile	Australia
Czech Republic	Denmark	France	Hungary[na]
Estonia	Norway	Mexico	Japan[na]
Finland	Korea		
Germany	Slovenia		
Ireland	Sweden		
Italy	Turkey		
Luxembourg			
New Zealand			
Spain			
Switzerland			
United Kingdom			
Non-OECD	**Non-OECD**		
South Africa	Philippines		

Note: Total respondents: 25, [na] not answered

Source: OECD (2016), OECD Survey of Infrastructure Governance

Table 3.16. Are projects subject to an assessment of their affordability for the users?

All projects	All projects above a threshold	Certain projects	None	Not relevant/ Others
Belgium	Denmark	Chile	Finland	Australia[1]
Ireland	Norway	Czech Republic	France	Austria
Italy	Korea	Estonia	Sweden	Germany
Luxembourg		Mexico	Turkey	
Spain		New Zealand	Japan[na]	
United Kingdom		Slovenia	Hungary[na]	
		Switzerland		
Non-OECD	**Non-OECD**			
South Africa	Philippines			

Note: Total respondents: 26, [na] not answered; (1) Regulators review the pricing from suppliers in the water, electricity and gas, but not in transport (except for PPPs).

Source: OECD (2016), OECD Survey of Infrastructure Governance

Box 3.3. Land value capture tools: efficient and equitable funding for urban infrastructure

The idea behind land value capture is that landowners should contribute to the funding of public actions that increase the value of their land. In line with this thinking, one of the recommendations of the Vancouver Plan of Action from Habitat I entails the "beneficiary pays" principle, according to which the beneficiaries of public investments that valorise their land should partly cover such costs or return their benefit to the public (UN, 1976).

Public infrastructure projects such as public spaces, facilities, and mass transportation networks typically increase the land values of surrounding areas (Higgins and Kanaroglou, 2016). Beyond that, land valorisation also occurs upon land conversion from rural to urban, or as a result of changes in zoning classifications for use and densification parameters. In all these cases, private landowners benefit from an "unearned increment" - that is, an increase in the value of their land which is not caused by their actions. By taxing the unearned increment, public authorities can partially fund or even fully recover the costs of infrastructure projects, which are often complex and expensive.

Several different land value capture instruments can be used to capture the unearned increment. For example: A pure land value tax, betterment contributions, developer exactions, impact fees, sale or transfer of development rights, public land leasehold, land readjustment or joint development schemes (see OECD, 2017, for details on their characteristics and the use across different OECD countries).

These tools have been adopted in countries as varied as the United States, Canada, Brazil, Colombia, Argentina, Ethiopia, Poland, the Netherlands, Korea, Japan, and many others. Some countries have experimented more, and with a more diverse array of tools, like the United States and Brazil, while others have concentrated efforts into one mechanism alone. For instance, Colombia has a longstanding tradition of betterment contributions (Smolka, 2013), while Korea has typically led urban development through land readjustment, and Japan uses joint development schemes and land sales to fund railway projects. The Netherlands, Hong Kong and Israel all have public land leasehold systems, but use them differently and for different goals (Bourassa and Hong, 2003). Only three OECD countries adopt a pure land tax, though - Estonia, Denmark and Australia (Blöchliger, 2015).

Land value capture instruments are useful tools to fund infrastructure projects, is it not advisable to use revenues from them to broadly fund public actions on a permanent basis. Only pure land tax and joint development schemes have the potential to create recurrent revenues. What is more, because many of those tools rely on land markets, revenue collection depends on market conditions that dictate land and real estate prices. In short, these tools are commonly subjected to market volatility, and as such may become somewhat unstable revenue sources.

> ## Box 3.3. Land value capture tools: Efficient and equitable funding for urban infrastructure *(cont.)*
>
> Successful implementation of land value capture tools requires technical capacity to regularly and accurately assess land values and increments, as well as alignment with spatial planning goals, and legal provisions. Yet, local initiatives have made successful implementation of land value capture mechanisms possible even where the institutional framework was challenging (Smolka, 2013). A good example is Trenque Lauquen in Argentina. The city was legally prohibited to raise local property taxes and so it adopted a betterment contribution to charge landowners for infrastructure works and planning decisions that cause land valorisation, with significant financial success (Duarte and Baer, 2013).
>
> Sources: Blöchliger, H. (2015), Reforming the Tax on Immovable Property: Taking Care of the Unloved, OECD Economics Department Working Papers, No. 1205, OECD Publishing, Paris http://dx.doi.org/10.1787/5js30tw0n7kg-en; Bourassa, S. C., & Hong, Y. H. (2003), Leasing public land: Policy Debates and International Experiences, Lincoln Institute of Land Policy; Duarte, J. I. and Baer, L. (2013), Recuperación de plusvalías a través de la contribución por mejoras en Trenque Lauquen, Provincia de Buenos Aires – Argentina, Working Paper, Lincoln Institute of Land Policy; Higgins, C. D. and Pavlos S. Kanaroglou (2016), Forty years of modelling rapid transit's land value uplift in North America: moving beyond the tip of the iceberg, Transport Reviews, 36:5, 610-634, DOI: 10.1080/01441647.2016.1174748; OECD (2017), Land-use planning systems in the OECD: Country Fact Sheets (forthcoming); Smolka, M. (2013), Implementing Value Capture in Latin America: Policies and Tools for Urban Development, Policy Focus Report Series, Lincoln Institute of Land Policy; UN (United Nations), (1976), The Vancouver Action Plan- Recommendation D.3., United Nations Conference on Human Settlement, Vancouver, Canada.

Determinants for project funding

A strong cost-benefit analysis result is the most important determinant to receive funding (Figure 3.7*)*. Similar to previous results, costs benefit analysis is an important tool for decisions on funding, followed by whether the project is part of the long term strategic plan. The overall third highest ranked criterion is strong political backing, followed by whether the project has a functional fit with other infrastructure assets. The importance for developing a particular sector, strong private sector interest, external funding from EU or other donors, strong market failures in the sector, and strong popular backing are ranked lower. These results correspond to the results of criteria for prioritisation.

Figure 3.7. What usually determines whether a project received funding/is approved for delivery?

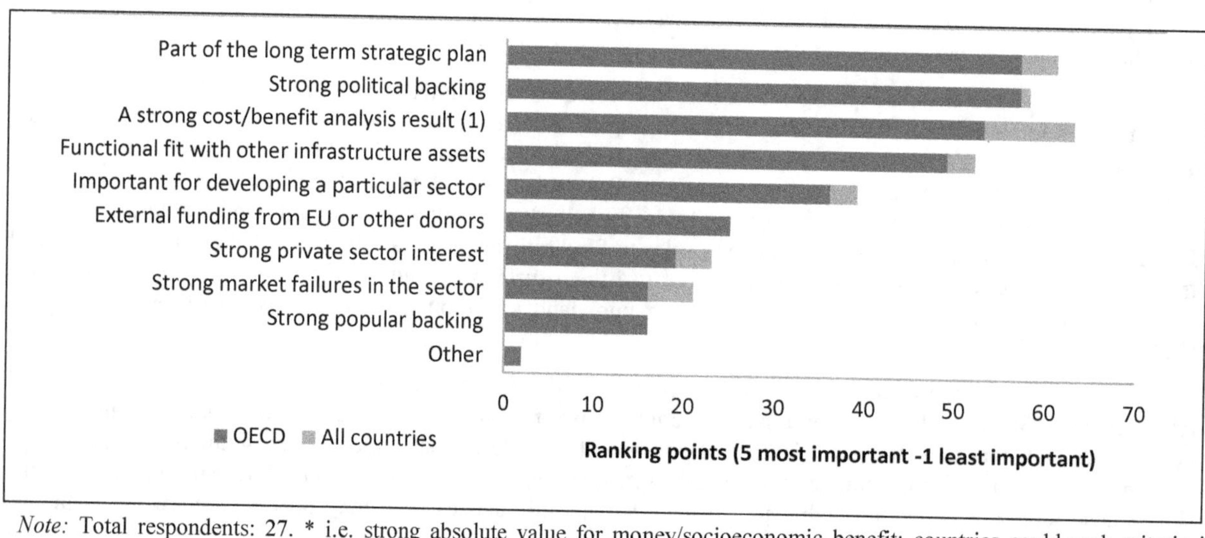

Note: Total respondents: 27. * i.e. strong absolute value for money/socioeconomic benefit; countries could rank criteria in declining importance (5 to 1 ranking points).
Source: OECD (2016), OECD Survey of Infrastructure Governance

Less than half of respondents have a procedure dedicated for identifying and allocating risks between public vs. private parties. It can be helpful in terms of VFM and affordability to assess the public-private participation mix. This, however, requires a sober assessment of the projects characteristic, including risks and uncertainties, and their pricing and allocation. An explicit procedure is in place for 10 examined countries, whereas 3 respondents have no concrete procedure but guidance or soft laws (others), or the procedure is only applied for PPPs (France and South Africa) (Table 3.17).

Table 3.17. Is there a dedicated procedure for identifying and allocating risks between public and private parties that take the cost of such allocation into account?

Yes	Yes, if PPP	No	Other
Australia	France	Austria	Japan
Czech Republic		Belgium	Italy
Germany		Chile	United Kingdom
Ireland		Denmark	
Mexico		Estonia	
New Zealand		Finland	
Norway		Hungary	
Korea		Luxembourg	
Switzerland		Slovenia	
		Spain	
Non-OECD	Non-OECD	Sweden	
Philippines	South Africa	Turkey	

Note: Total respondents: 27

Source: OECD (2016), OECD Survey of Infrastructure Governance

The choice of particular delivery modalities may be motivated by the wish to finance the project in a non-transparent manner. Sometimes a delivery modality, especially the use of PPPs, is chosen to avoid fiscal rules on the government's debt and deficits, rather than because of cost efficiency. In about half of the responding countries, the full costs of the asset is budgeted upfront, regardless of how it is implemented (Table 3.18), deleting any particular budgetary advantage of non-user financed PPPs. Furthermore, while for public works the financing is included in the relevant budget (national, sub-national), for a significant share of SOEs and PPPs or concessions it is not or only for certain elements (Figure 3.8).

Table 3.18. In your country, is the full cost of the asset budgeted upfront regardless of how it is implemented?

Yes	No
Australia	Austria
Chile	Belgium
Czech Republic	Denmark
Finland	Estonia
France	Ireland
Germany	Italy
Luxembourg	Korea
Mexico	Slovenia
New Zealand	Turkey
Norway	Switzerland

Table 3.18. In your country, is the full cost of the asset budgeted upfront regardless of how it is implemented? *(cont.)*

Yes	No
Sweden	Hungary[na]
Spain	Japan[na]
United Kingdom	
Non-OECD	**Non-OECD**
South Africa	Philippines

Note: Total respondents: 25, [na] not answered
Source: OECD (2016), OECD Survey of Infrastructure Governance

Figure 3.8. Is the financing of the delivery types below include in the budget of the relevant (national, sub-national) government level?

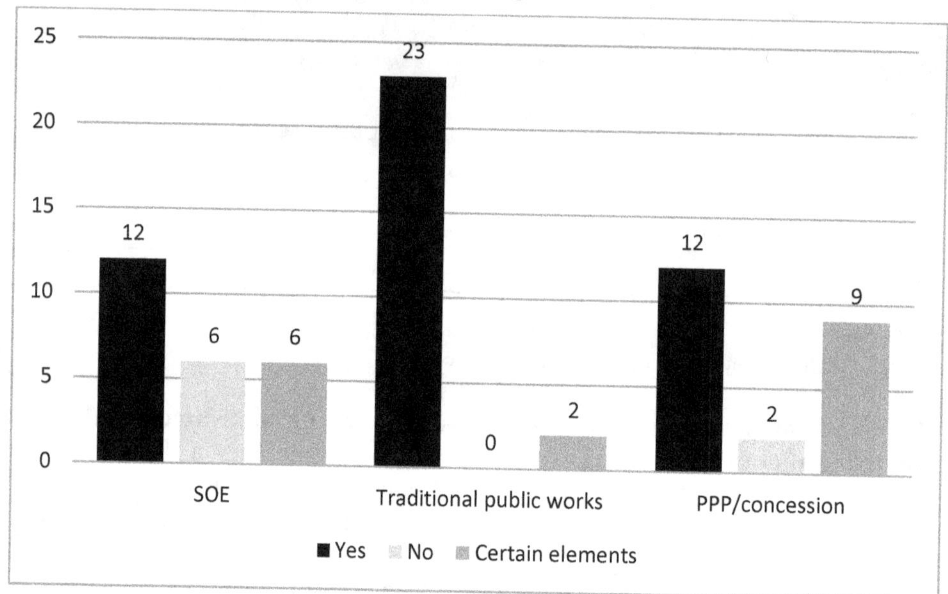

Note: Total respondents: 27
Source: OECD (2016), OECD Survey of Infrastructure Governance

Accounting rules can create incentives. This is especially important in terms of whether certain assets, such as PPPs should be on or off the government's budget sheet. The case that some countries may not report the assets and liabilities on the balance sheet could be explained by technical difficulties for inventorying contracts and evaluating the related debt, or implementing the control approach required by international standards, as in Chile.

In most of the cases, contingent liabilities and running costs are listed and priced, although it is slightly less common for PPP or concessions and SOEs than for public works (Figure 3.9). For PPP projects the number of countries accounting for contingent liabilities and running costs has increased to 10[15] countries in comparison to the results in Hawkesworth and Burger (2013), that listed only four countries - and in only three countries for SOEs, agencies and private incorporated businesses - that list and price contingent liabilities. Ideally they should be listed and priced, but merely listing them would help to highlight potential problems, as done in Australia, Finland, France and Philippines.

Figure 3.9. Does the budget documentation or other published material contain an assessment with respect to contingent liabilities derived from:

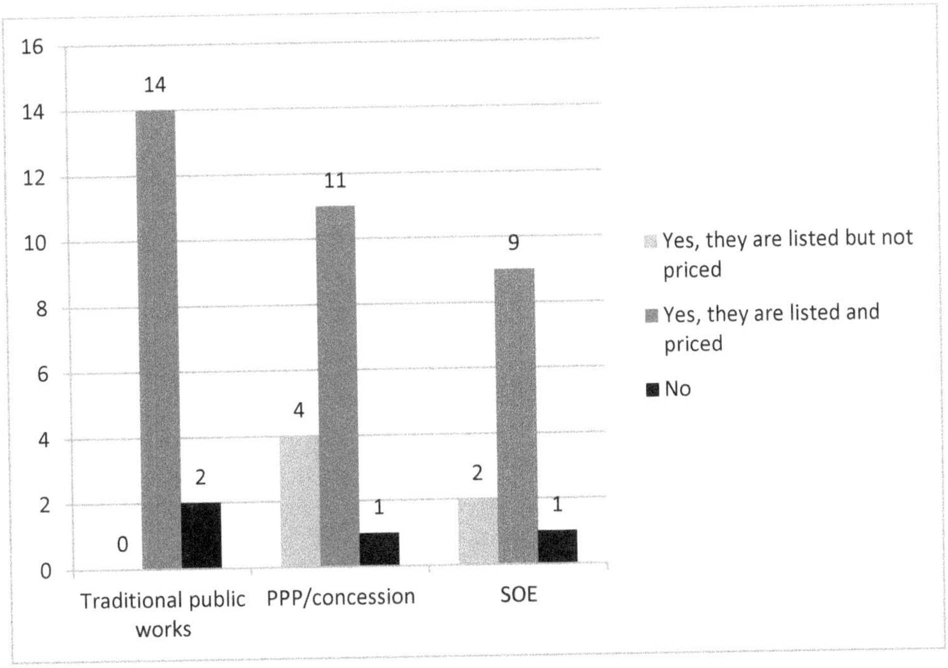

Note: Total respondents: 20
Source: OECD (2016), OECD Survey of Infrastructure Governance

Table 3.19. Does the budget documentation or other published material contain an assessment with respect to contingent liabilities derived from (2013):

	PPPs	SOEs, agencies and private incorporated businesses
Yes, they are listed but not priced	3 (Canada, Italy and South Africa)	3 (Canada, Italy and South Africa
Yes, they are listed and priced	4 (Czech Republic, Estonia, Finland and the Slovak Republic)	3 (Canada, Italy and New Zealand)
No	11	11

Source: Table 14 in Burger, Philippe and Ian Hawkesworth (2013), "Capital budgeting and procurement practices", *OECD Journal on Budgeting*, Vol. 13/1. http://dx.doi.org/10.1787/budget-13-5k3w580lh1q7

The study shows due to the widely applied European standards, the risk approach in accounting assets is more common. All EU-members represented in the survey use the Eurostat criteria for their accounting, which present a risk approach to accounting (Table 3.20). A similar approach is used in the Philippines and Turkey, where the accounting is based on whether the party carries the majority of the risk. Fewer countries, apply the control approach, as required in international accounting standards (IFRS or IPSAS), basing the accounting on whether the party has the control over the asset. The Norwegian government accounts are cash based and infrastructure assets are not activated in the accounts, whereas all investments, except from some investments made by SOEs, are included in the government budget and the investment expenditures are also included in the government accounts. The use of both approaches in one country can be attributed to different government levels.

Table 3.20. Approaches used to decide whether or not an asset involved in a private finance type/PPP project is included in the government accounts?

Control approach	Risk approach
Austria*	Austria×
Chile*	Belgium×
Korea*	Czech Republic×
Slovenia*	Denmark×
Turkey*	Estonia×
Switzerland*	Finland×
Ireland	France×
Mexico	Germany×
	Ireland×
	Italy×
	Luxembourg×
	Slovenia×
	Spain×
	Sweden×
	United Kingdom×
	Turkey
Non-OECD	**Non-OECD**
Philippines*	South Africa
	Philippines

Note: Total respondents: 27, none: Australia, Others: Norway, *International accounting standards (IFRS or IPSAS), ×Eurostat criteria

Source: OECD (2016), OECD Survey of Infrastructure Governance

In 21 out of 26 countries the Central Budget Authority (CBA) has a formal gate-keeping role in approving infrastructure projects (Table 3.21). This means that in most countries if approval by the CBA is not obtained, the project cannot proceed. Survey results show that the criteria used by the CBA for the approval of infrastructure projects and assuring their affordability focus on the projects affordability for both the national budget and users, value for money, and to a lesser extent on the presence of mandated documentation for all projects (Figure 3.10).

Table 3.21. Does the Central Budget Authority have a formal, gate-keeping role in approving infrastructure projects?

Yes	No
Austria	Australia
Belgium	Estonia
Chile	New Zealand
Czech Republic	Norway
Denmark	Switzerland
Finland	Hungary [na]
France	
Germany	
Ireland	

Table 3.21. Does the Central Budget Authority have a formal, gate-keeping role in approving infrastructure projects? *(cont.)*

Yes	No
Italy	
Japan	
Luxembourg	
Mexico	
Korea	
Slovenia	
Spain	
Sweden	
Turkey	
United Kingdom	
Non-OECD	
Philippines	
South Africa	

Note: Total respondents: 26, [na] not answered

Source: OECD (2016), OECD Survey of Infrastructure Governance

Figure 3.10. What are the criteria used by the Central Budget Authority for the approval of infrastructure projects?

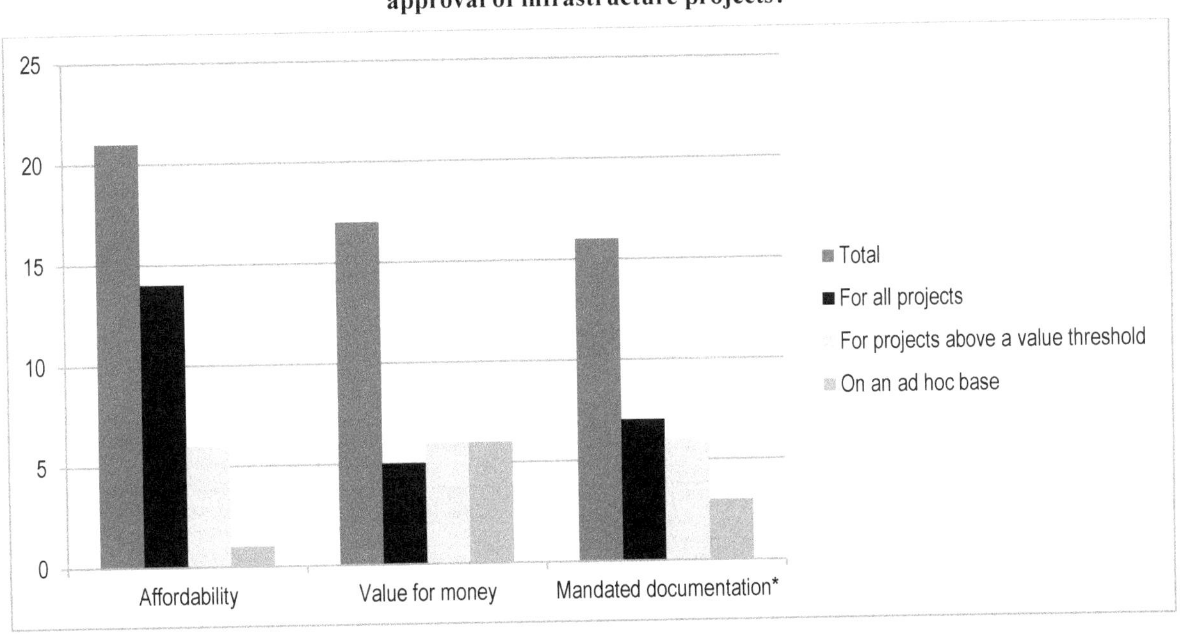

Note: Total respondents: 21 (Countries where the Central Budget Authority has a formal, gate-keeping role in approving infrastructure projects), * including elements such as environmental impact, cost-benefit analysis, write-up of stakeholder consultation.

Source: OECD (2016), OECD Survey of Infrastructure Governance

Tendering and contracting

Strong competition is necessary for ensuring value for money from tendering. This however, can be at times difficult to achieve. In response, 22 of the countries have a strategy in place that aims at ensuring a competitive tendering process (Table 3.22*)*.

Practically all respondents have specific conditions under which the statutory thresholds for tendering apply. Almost in equal parts the conditions are according to EU regulation (10) or national regulation (12) (including national regulations based on EU-regulations). Only New Zealand has no clear set of conditions (Table 3.23).

Table 3.22. Is there a strategy or policy in place that works towards ensuring a competitive tendering process?

Yes	No
Australia	Estonia
Austria	Finland
Belgium	Turkey
Chile	Japan[na]
Czech Republic	Slovenia[na]
Denmark	
France	
Germany	
Hungary	
Ireland	
Italy	
Luxembourg	
Mexico	
New Zealand	
Norway	
Korea	
Spain	
Sweden	
Switzerland	
United Kingdom	
Non-OECD	
Philippines	
South Africa	

Note: Total respondents: 25, [na] not answered
Source: OECD (2016), OECD Survey of Infrastructure Governance

Table 3.23. Is there a clear set of conditions specified under which the statutory threshold for tender applies?

Yes, according to national regulation	Yes, according to EU regulation	No	Other
Chile	Austria	New Zealand	Australia[1]
Estonia	Belgium	Hungary[na]	Switzerland[2]
France	Czech Republic	Japan[na]	
Italy	Denmark		
Luxembourg	Finland		
Mexico	Germany		

**Table 3.23. Is there a clear set of conditions specified under which
the statutory threshold for tender applies?** *(cont.)*

Yes, according to national regulation	Yes, according to EU regulation	No	Other
Korea	Ireland		
Slovenia	Norway		
Turkey	Spain		
United Kingdom	Sweden		
Non-OECD			
Philippines			
South Africa			

Note: Total respondents: 25, [na] not answered, 1. The Australian Government is not involved in tenders, which is a state/territory government issue. 2. World Trade Organisation Agreement on Government Procurement (GPA)

Source: OECD (2016), OECD Survey of Infrastructure Governance

Open tendering is the most probable form of tendering, mostly depending on a sufficient level of competition and the need for increased innovation (*Figure 11*). Open tendering is the most open procurement process, in which any company which considers itself being able to respond can participate. The likeliness of using an open tender process depends on the wish to ensure a sufficient level of competition, but also on political, sectoral sensitivity and the tradition in the sector for a certain tendering form. The need for innovation, which is not as important for the choice for open tendering, makes less open forms such as selective tendering and negotiated tendering relatively more probable. Unknown parameters of the output increase the likeliness of choosing a two-stage tendering[16] form. Other forms include project or sector specific processes.

Figure 3.11. Please specify which of the listed criteria make the below forms of tendering more probable

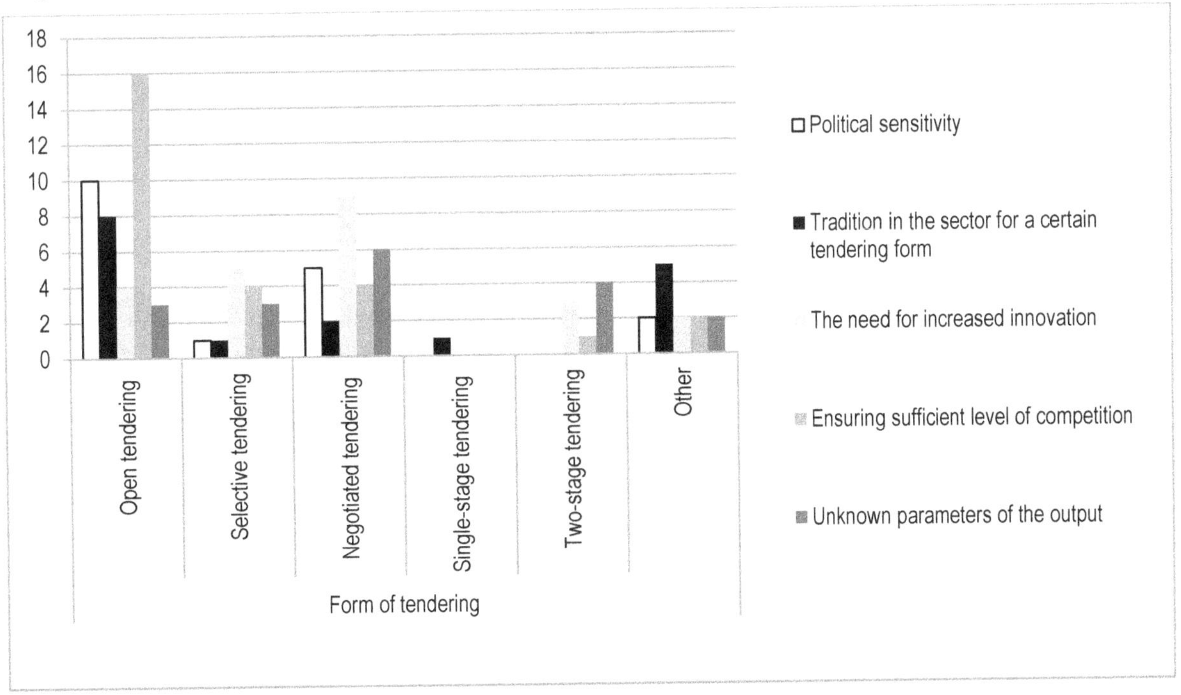

Note: Total respondents: 27

Source: OECD (2016), OECD Survey of Infrastructure Governance

More than half of the countries feel that there are sufficient resources to ensure value for money from the contract (Table 3.24). In the preparation and phases, there need to be sufficient public sector resources to ensure accountability and value for money. This is met by 16 of the countries.

Table 3.24. In general, is there a dedicated function/policy allocating sufficient resources and monitoring capacity ensuring value for money in contracting?

Yes	No	Other
Australia[4]	Austria	Belgium[1]
Czech Republic	Estonia	Chile[2]
Denmark	Germany	
Finland	Italy	
France	New Zealand	
Ireland	Slovenia	
Luxembourg	Switzerland	
Mexico	Hungary[na]	
Norway	Japan[na]	
Korea		
Spain		
Sweden		
Turkey		
United Kingdom		
Non-OECD		
Philippines		
South Africa		

Note: Total respondents: 25, [na] not answered; (1) Administrative and budgetary control;(2) On a need-to-need-basis; (3) For PPPs only; (4) Missing resources for planning at sub-national level.

Source: OECD (2016), OECD Survey of Infrastructure Governance

Generation, analysis and disclosure of data

Good infrastructure policy should be based on data. Governments should put in place systems that ensure a systematic collection of relevant data and institutional responsibility for analysis, dissemination, and learning from this data. Relevant data should be disclosed to the public in an accessible format and in a timely fashion.

The lack of data on the other hand makes it difficult evaluate and monitor the projects' performance and to base future decision and delivery modalities and contracts on comparable data and information. Additionally, to enhance transparency and confidence among the stakeholder, the government should disclose key data to the public.

Systematic data collection on the infrastructure asset's performance is infrequent. Eight of the respondents have a central, systematic and formal collection of information on financial and non-financial performance of the infrastructure projects (Table 3.25). This low number makes it harder to compare various forms of infrastructure delivery models. If however, such a collection is in place, most information is collected by the Central Infrastructure Unit, followed by the dedicated PPP units or line ministries (Figure 3.12). According to the respondents the data collected includes data on: The physical progress, financial progress, tenders and contracts, variations with respect to planned progress, economic performance, and accuracy of the original cost-benefit analysis, among others.

Table 3.25. Is there a central, systematic and formal collection of information on financial and non-financial performance of infrastructure that makes it possible to compare various forms of infrastructure delivery models?

Yes	No
Australia	Austria
Finland	Belgium
Japan	Chile
Mexico	Czech Republic
New Zealand	Denmark
Korea	Estonia
Spain	France
	Germany
	Ireland
	Italy
	Luxembourg
	Norway[1]
	Slovenia
	Sweden
	Turkey
	Switzerland
	United Kingdom
	Hungary[na]
Non-OECD	**Non-OECD**
Philippines	South Africa

Note: Total respondents: 27, [na] not answered, (1) In Norway, the *concept research programme* will collect financial information and some other key information for all projects in a projects database (trailbase) above NOK 750 mill. (about EUR 80 mill). The database is not public, but is available for government institutions, researchers on requests. The research programme publishes comparative reports based on these data from time to time and these reports are publically available.

Source: OECD (2016), OECD Survey of Infrastructure Governance

Figure 3.12. Who collects information on financial and non-financial performance of infrastructure?

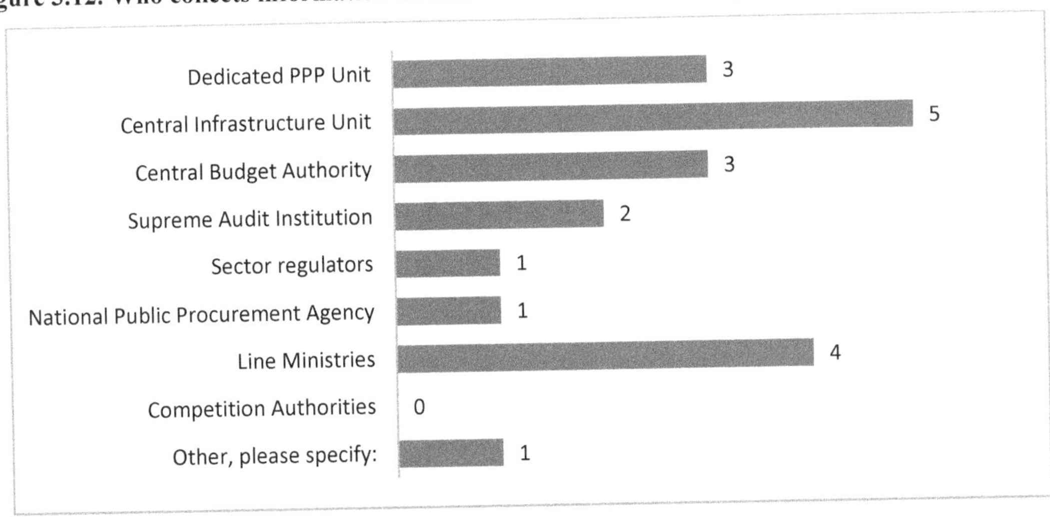

Note: Total respondents: 8 (Countries with a central, systematic and formal collection of information).

Source: OECD (2016), OECD Survey of Infrastructure Governance

Disclosure of infrastructure data is limited. Systematic disclosure of *ex ante* data of infrastructure projects during the preparation phase is established in 12[17] countries. Disclosure of performance data is equally rare. In 9 of the countries with a formal policy ensuring that the relevant authority conducts assessments of each project authorities, the authority   published performance data partially, in 2 countries authorities made performance information fully available to the public (Table 3.26). Although there is no formal policy ensuring performance assessment in Norway, evaluations reports of some infrastructure projects in operation are publically available on a common evaluation portal.

Table 3.26. Is the performance information available for the public?

Fully[1]	Partially	Not available
United Kingdom	France	Czech Republic
	Germany	Turkey
	Italy	Finland
	Japan	
	Mexico	
	Philippines	
	Korea	
	Spain	
Non-OECD	**Non-OECD**	
Philippines	South Africa	

Note: Total respondents: 13 (Countries with a formal policy ensuring that the relevant line ministry or agency conducts performance assessment of each project and France), naming 17 authorities collecting data. 1. At least one authority discloses the information fully.

Source: OECD (2016), OECD Survey of Infrastructure Governance

Data on public investment flows and stocks are available in more than half of the countries. Eighteen countries have data on infrastructure investment flows, seventeen on stock (Table 3.27). For the respondents with flow data available, sectorial breakdown are also available, especially for water (17) and air transportation (Table 3.28). In the case of stock data, sectorial breakdown is especially available for railway, road and air transportation (Table 3.29).

Table 3.27. Does your country have the following information for infrastructure investment?

Infrastructure investment flow data	Infrastructure investment stock data
Australia[1]	Australia[1]
Austria	Austria
Chile	Denmark
Czech Republic	Estonia
Denmark	Finland
Finland	France
France	Germany
Germany	Italy
Italy	Korea
Korea	Mexico
Mexico	New Zealand
New Zealand	Norway
Norway	Spain

Table 3.27. Does your country have the following information for infrastructure investment? *(cont.)*

Infrastructure investment flow data	Infrastructure investment stock data
Slovenia	Sweden
Spain	Switzerland
Sweden	Turkey
Switzerland	United Kingdom
Turkey	
United Kingdom	

Note: Total respondents: 27; (1) Partially, the Australian federal government does not have collated data on infrastructure investment flow or stock data as this is managed by state and local governments. The Federal Government records and reports on its own investments in state/local government infrastructure. Publicly owned assets proposed for sale or lease are listed on the National Infrastructure Construction Schedule website (https://www.nics.gov.au/AssetSales/AssetSale).

Source: OECD (2016), OECD Survey of Infrastructure Governance

Table 3.28. Countries with flow data in a sectorial breakdown

Electricity	Gas	Water	Railway transportation	Road transportation	Water transportation	Air transportation	Tele-communications
Austria	Austria	Austria	Austria	Austria	Austria	Austria	Austria
Chile	Chile	Chile	Czech Republic	Czech Republic	Chile	Chile	Chile
Finland	Finland	Czech Republic	Denmark	Denmark	Czech Republic	Czech Republic	Finland
France	France	Finland	Finland	Finland	Finland	Finland	France
Italy	Italy	France	France	France	France	France	Germany
Korea	Korea	Germany	Korea	Korea	Germany	Germany	Italy
Mexico	Mexico	Italy	Mexico	Mexico	Korea	Korea	Korea
New Zealand	New Zealand	Korea	New Zealand	New Zealand	Mexico	Mexico	Mexico
Norway	Norway	Mexico	Norway	Norway	New Zealand	New Zealand	New Zealand
Sweden	Sweden	New Zealand	Slovenia	Slovenia	Norway	Norway	Norway
Switzerland	Switzerland	Norway	Spain	Spain	Spain	Slovenia	Slovenia
Turkey	Turkey	Slovenia	Sweden	Sweden	Sweden	Spain	Sweden
United Kingdom	United Kingdom	Spain	Switzerland	Switzerland	Switzerland	Sweden	Switzerland
		Sweden	Turkey	Turkey	Turkey	Switzerland	Turkey
		Switzerland	United Kingdom	United Kingdom		Turkey	United Kingdom
		Turkey				United Kingdom	
		United Kingdom					

Note: Total respondents: 18

Source: OECD (2016), OECD Survey of Infrastructure Governance

Table 3.29. Countries with stock data in a sectorial breakdown

Electricity	Gas	Water	Railway transportation	Road transportation	Water transportation	Air transportation	Tele-communications
Austria	Austria	Austria	Austria	Austria	Austria	Austria	Austria
Estonia	Estonia	Finland	Denmark	Denmark	Estonia	Estonia	Finland
Finland	Finland	France	Estonia	Estonia	Finland	Finland	France
France	France	Germany	Finland	Finland	France	France	Germany
Korea	Korea	Korea	France	France	Germany	Germany	Korea
Mexico	Mexico	Mexico	Italy	Italy	Korea	Italy	Mexico
New Zealand	New Zealand	New Zealand	Korea	Korea	Mexico	Korea	New Zealand
Norway	Norway	Norway	Mexico	Mexico	New Zealand	Mexico	Norway
Switzerland	Switzerland	Spain	New Zealand	New Zealand	Norway	New Zealand	Switzerland
Turkey	Turkey	Switzerland	Norway	Norway	Spain	Norway	Turkey
United Kingdom	United Kingdom	Turkey	Spain	Spain	Turkey	Spain	United Kingdom
		United Kingdom	Sweden	Sweden		Switzerland	
			Switzerland	Switzerland		Turkey	
			Turkey	Turkey		United Kingdom	
			United Kingdom	United Kingdom			

Note: Total respondents: 16

Source: OECD (2016), OECD Survey of Infrastructure Governance

Performance throughout the life-cycle

Ensure a focus on the performance of the asset throughout its lifespan by putting in place monitoring systems and institutions.

The monitoring during the operational phase includes regular observation and recording of the performance data of the asset on all aspects relevant to the procurement of the infrastructure service to the public and users. Monitoring serves to ensure value for money and to manage risks throughout the operational phase. The responsibility for this should lie with the central agencies, such as the Central Budget Authority, Supreme Audit Institution and regulatory authorities.

Performance assessment is mandated in about half of the countries. Of all examined countries, 14 have a policy ensuring an assessment of the performance of each project (Table 3.30). In 8 of those cases, the policy is centrally mandated, whereas for 6 it is the line department's responsibility to decide upon such a policy.

Table 3.30. Is there a formal policy ensuring that the relevant line ministry or agency conducts performance assessment of each project?

Yes	No
Czech Republic	Australia
Finland	Austria
Germany	Belgium
Ireland	Chile
Italy	Denmark
Japan	Estonia
Mexico	France
New Zealand	Luxembourg
Korea	Norway
Spain	Slovenia

Table 3.30. Is there a formal policy ensuring that the relevant line ministry or agency conducts performance assessment of each project? *(cont.)*

Yes	No
Turkey	Sweden
United Kingdom	Switzerland
	Hungary[na]
Non-OECD	**Non-OECD**
Philippines	South Africa

Note: Total respondents: 26, [na] not answered

Source: OECD (2016), OECD Survey of Infrastructure Governance

The most common form of audits by the Supreme Audit Institution regarding infrastructure assets is on case by case basis. The Supreme Audit Institution should audit and assess individual projects as well as the infrastructure programme in general with regards to its finance, performance, value for money finance and compliance over the life-cycle. This *ex post* evaluation demands enough human and financial resources and dedicated tools. Systematic audits are also common for financial audits but less used with respect to value for money. Other types of audits include resilience to climate change and disasters, and clearances attesting the implementation readiness of the agency (Figure 3.13).

Figure 3.13. What type of audits does the Supreme Audit Institution perform regarding infrastructure assets?

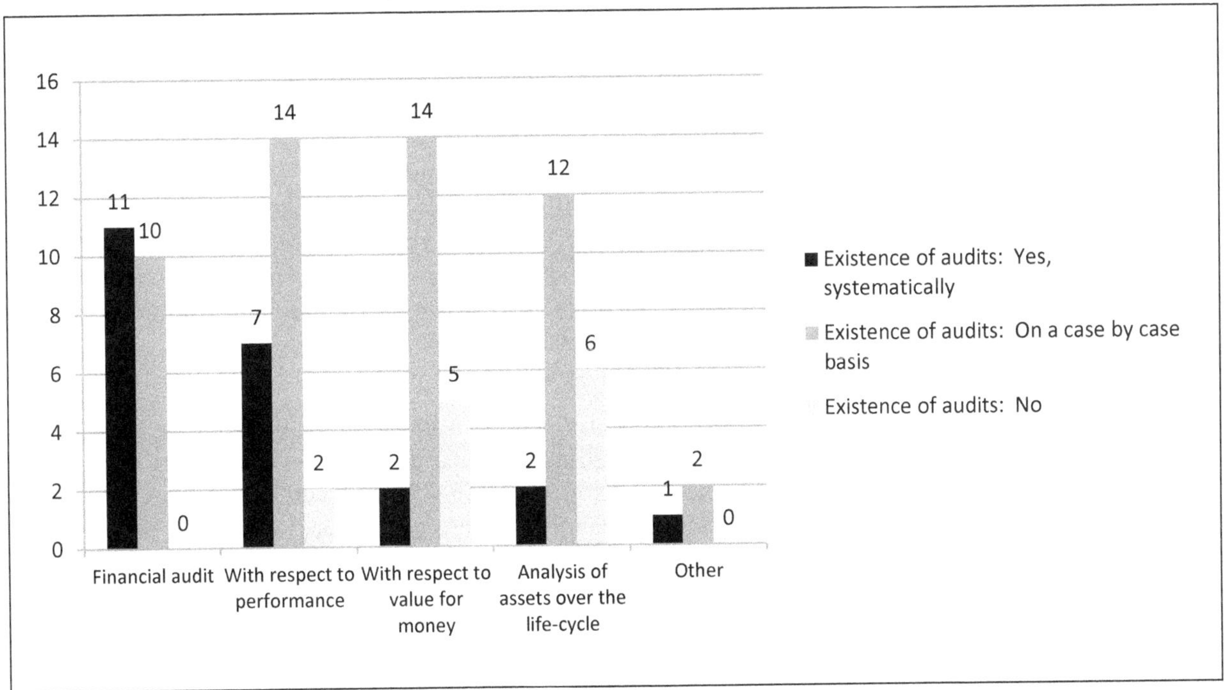

Note: Total respondents: 27

Source: OECD (2016), OECD Survey of Infrastructure Governance

With both private and public parties involved in the project, external shocks are the main reason for renegotiation in during the projects life-cycle. The long-term nature and high uncertainty of infrastructure projects makes renegotiations of contracts with the private sector very likely. Contractual arrangement should therefore clearly specify the mechanisms and conditions of re-negotiations in long term agreements. Special care should be given to the conservation of value for money during renegotiation. Only if conditions change due to discretionary public policy actions should the government consider compensating the private sector. The data shows that the most common reason for re-negotiating is a change in conditions to discretionary public policy actions (10) or external shocks (9). Other reasons include changes in original conditions (Chile), and renegotiation under the operational efficiency savings programme (United Kingdom). Norway has a system for taking in amendments in the contracts if necessary.

Concluding summary of the survey results

The analysis shows that for some dimensions good practices are common among the set of countries examined. However, other practices suggested by the framework are less present and demand attention. In general no best practice country group can be identified which reflects the importance of improving infrastructure governance across countries.

A deficit can be identified with the establishment of **long term strategies**. Only 13 of the 27 examined countries have a long term vision in form of a long term plan across sectors. Most of the remaining countries have only sectoral plans, missing chances for synergies, complementarities and co-ordination. On medium term, 17 of the respondents have a clear prioritised short list of projects. Motivations for long term strategies and prioritisation are heterogeneous across countries. In several countries these long term plans are updated by fixed time intervals, but in an equal amount of cases, this decision is based on political considerations.

The most relevant criteria **determining the delivery modality** are financial criteria, such as public sector financial resources, availability of public sector capacity, the wish to tab private finance sources to augment the pubic budget, cost recovery possible from users, as well as the outcome of a quantitative analysis. Strong results from a cost-benefit analysis are also the strongest argument for projects to be shortlisted. However, projects move from the short list to implementation based on political considerations. The decision for public procurement is often based on habit.

Many essential **regulatory** processes for good infrastructure governance are formalised in most countries and are perceived as effective. Nevertheless, the roles and capacities of regulators are often unclear and co-ordination is lacking. In 24 countries the line ministries are the institutions in charge of infrastructure governance. Dedicated units on the other hand are less common, such as Supreme Audit Institutions or PPP Units.

Mandatory **consultation processes** are widely used across the countries. Especially regarding the long-term strategic plan it is widespread to have a public consultation. However, consultation takes mainly places during the infrastructure project preparation and to a lesser extent during construction or for the evaluation of infrastructure needs. Procedure to specifically identify users' needs is only mandatory in 11 countries.

Co-ordinated across levels of governments is common in countries with long term strategic plans. However, in general few central units aim to strengthen the capacities of sub-national governments. Intergovernmental co-ordination mechanisms for infrastructure are in place for a little more than half of the countries in the survey.

Affordability is an important factor when it comes to the decision whether and how an infrastructure project will be delivered. An assessment of the affordability for the public budget is in place in the majority of the countries. Strong, absolute as well as relative value for money results are the most important criteria for the project's approval and funding. Cost-benefit analysis is the most popular approach to determine absolute value for money.

Only in half of the countries, the full costs of the asset are **budgeted upfront**, regardless of how it is implemented. This however, is important to avoid that the choice of particular delivery modalities may be motivated by the wish to finance the project in a non-transparent manner. Transparency about the cost of the asset is furthermore assured by accounting for future costs and liabilities a priori. Twenty countries have formal requirements in place to account for running costs and contingent liabilities associated with an infrastructure asset. However, only less than half of respondents have a procedure dedicated for identifying and allocating risks between public and private parties.

Systematic **data collection** on the infrastructure asset's performance is infrequent. Disclosure of infrastructure data is limited. The lack of data impedes to evaluate and monitor the projects' performance and to base future decision and delivery modalities and contracts on comparable data and information.

Governance throughout the life cycle needs to be improved. Most institutions are responsible for the development of infrastructure policy and the improvement of infrastructure performance. Responsibilities for the assessment and monitoring of the projects are less defined. Performance assessment for example is only mandated in half of the countries and audits by the Supreme Audit Institution regarding infrastructure assets are mainly conducted on case by case basis.

A majority of all respondents have an explicit policy in place that regulates conflicts of interest in the tender panel, as well as formal appeal mechanisms in the tendering process. Specific measures against **corruption and integrity threats** in infrastructure on the other hand are only applied in half of the countries.

Notes

1. 2016 Survey of Infrastructure Governance

2. Missing answers may be due to inapplicability or missing data.

3. If nor otherwise indicated, the number in brackets refers to the number of countries.

4. Telecom, air transport, energy, hydraulic, health, tourism, urban development and housing infrastructure

5. No answer by Japan

6. Either long term, medium term, regional or sectorial.

7. A similar long term plan exists for Defence. The plan is revised every 4th year, but has a longer perspective, looking approximately 20 year ahead.

8. Representing 8 countries.

9. A maximum of 4 institutions per country could be listed.

10. Australia, Austria, Denmark, France, Germany, Greece*, Ireland, Korea, Netherlands*, South Africa, United Kingdom. Canada, Italy, Mexico follow this

practice in most of the cases (> 50% of the time but less than 100%). Countries marked with an asterisk did not participate in the presented 2016 study.

11.   Mexico, Slovenia, Turkey, Philippines, South Africa, Sweden, Chile

12.   In New Zealand the plan refers to infrastructure related to central government, local government and the private sector.

13.   These results are slightly different to the results found in Burger and Hawkesworth (2011): in the paper Australia, Austria, Canada, Denmark, Germany, and the United Kingdom stated to conduct a process to ascertain value for money ex ante for all PPPs and TIPs.

14.   Australia, Philippines, New Zealand, South Africa, Japan, Hungary, Belgium

15.   Czech Republic, Germany, Ireland, Korea, Luxembourg, Slovenia, South Africa, Spain, Turkey, United Kingdom

16.   Only companies qualified in the 1st round can compete in the 2nd round.

17.   Czech Republic, Denmark, Italy, Mexico, New Zealand, Norway, Philippines, Republic of Korea, Slovenia, Spain, Turkey, United Kingdom

Bibliography

Burger, P. and Hawkesworth, I. (2011), "How To Attain Value for Money: Comparing PPP and Traditional Infrastructure Public Procurement", *OECD Journal on Budgeting*, Volume 2011/1, OECD Publishing, Paris, http://dx.doi.org/10.1787/budget-11-5kg9zc0pvq6j

Burger, Philippe and Ian Hawkesworth (2013), "Capital budgeting and procurement practices", OECD Journal on Budgeting, Vol. 13/1, http://dx.doi.org/10.1787/budget-13-5k3w580lh1q7

ANNEX A

Key relevant OECD Recommendations

<table>
<tr><td>

Box A1.
Key relevant OECD Recommendations that inform this work

- OECD (2016) Integrity Framework for Public Investment

- OECD (2015) Towards a Framework for the Governance of Infrastructure

- OECD (2015) Recommendation of the Council on Public Procurement

- OECD (2015) Recommendation of the Council on Budgetary governance

- OECD (2015) High-Level Principles for Integrity, Transparency and Effective Control of Major Events and Related Large Infrastructure

- OECD (2014) Recommendation of the Council on Digital Government Strategies

- OECD (2014) Recommendation of the Council on Effective Public Investment Across Levels of Government

- OECD (2014), The Governance of Regulators, OECD Best-Practice Principles for Regulatory Policy

- OECD (2014) Recommendation of the Council on the Governance of Critical Risks

- OECD (2013) G20/OECD High-level principles of long term investment financing by Institutional investors

- OECD (2012) Recommendation of the Council for the Public Governance of Public-Private Partnerships

- OECD (2012) Recommendation of the Council on Regulatory Policy and Governance

- OECD (2010) Guiding Principles on Open and Inclusive Policy making

- OECD (2010) Recommendation of the Council on Principles for Transparency and Integrity in Lobbying

- OECD (2007) Recommendation of the Council on Principles for Private Participation in Infrastructure

- OECD (2003) Recommendation of the Council on OECD Guidelines for Managing Conflict of Interest in the Public Service

- OECD (1998) Recommendation of the Council on Improving Ethical Conduct in the Public Service Including Principles for Managing Ethics in the Public Service

</td></tr>
</table>

ANNEX B

Modality choice for infrastructure projects

Figure B1. The decision tree for modality choice

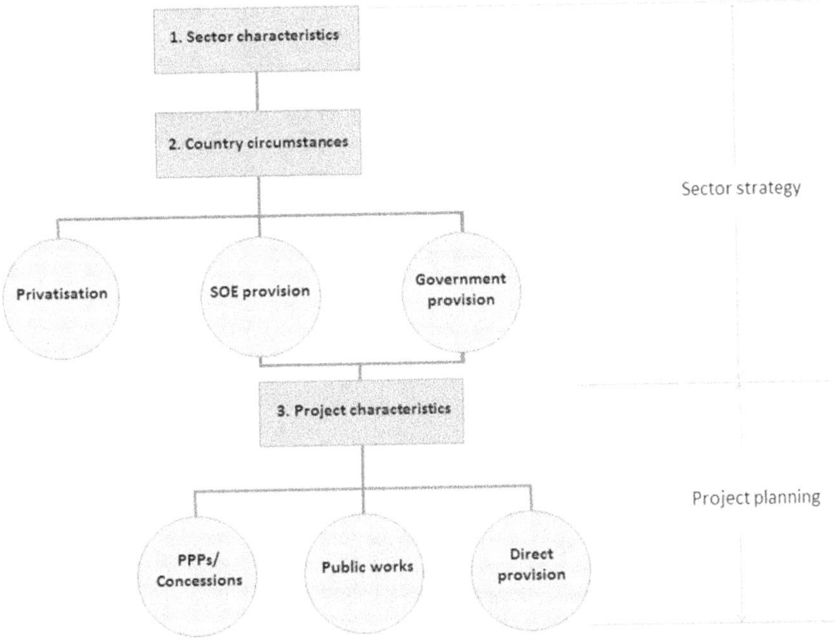

Box B1.
Check list for investigating relevant delivery mode (TIP vs. PPP)

Project size and profile

- Large initial capital outlay and long payback period?
- Is the project large enough to justify the additional legal, technical and financial costs of a PPP?
- Can quality enhancements in the design and construction phase generate savings during the operating phase of the project?
- Do these savings justify the additional transaction costs involved in bundling construction, operation and maintenance in a single contract?

Revenues and usage

- Can user fees be charged, are they affordable for the majority of users, and are they politically acceptable?
- Are user fees sufficient to cover the majority of capital and operating costs?
- Can usage be monitored?
- Quality
- Can the quantity and quality of project inputs be specified and measured efficiently?
- Will design innovation be required to achieve improvements in efficiency and value-for-money?

Box B1.
Check list for investigating relevant delivery mode (TIP vs. PPP) *(cont.)*

Uncertainty

- What is the level of uncertainty relating to future technological or societal conditions?

Risks

- How are risks allocated?
- Is demand relatively predictable over the lifetime of the project?
- Who is best placed to influence demand for the infrastructure-based service?
- Is the private sector willing to and capable of bearing some or all of the demand risk?
- Are there particular integrity risks in terms of corruption and undue influence that merit attention?

ANNEX C

Infrastructure deliveries

Box C1. Infrastructure ownership and delivery

There are many of ways to provide infrastructure services. The public sector's role can vary and there are a number of hybrid forms. The below list is therefore not exhaustive.

Infrastructure ownership

Government provision

Direct provision of infrastructure involves the government taking responsibility for all aspects of infrastructure delivery, including financing, construction, and subsequent service delivery. This mode affords the government a maximum level of control over the infrastructure asset.

State-owned enterprises (SOEs)

Infrastructure, particularly in network industries such as water, public transport and electricity, is often provided by SOEs that are fully or partially owned by the government. The government may relinquish infrastructure investments to an SOE if the latter is able to raise finance independently, although the actual investment decision may still be subject to government control if it has fiscal implications.

Privatisation

Under privatisation, private firms are not only responsible for the financing and delivery of infrastructure, but they also make investment decisions relating to which infrastructure assets to build. When privatisation has been the preferred option in sectors with potential market failures, governments have strengthened regulatory oversight in the sector at stake; this has been notably the case with the establishment of independent regulators in the energy and water sectors when systems have been privatised.

Infrastructure delivery modes

Design–Bid–Build

The project owner completes the majority of design work (sometimes with the assistance of specialised consultants). The project owner engages contractor(s) to build, based on supplied design. Risks associated with design faults, changing requirements and adverse site conditions are typically borne by the project owner.

Design–Build

The project owner only provides a project brief in the tender documentation, sometimes with only performance-based requirements. The contractor engages design consultants and bid on their developed design and lump sum construction price. Risks associated with errors or omissions in final design, and latent conditions are typically borne by contractors and design consultants. Costs of direct variation are typically borne by the project owner.

Box C1. Infrastructure ownership and delivery *(cont.)*

Construction management or general contractor

The contractor undertakes significant part of project management role, including: obtaining development approvals,   undertaking onsite investigations, finalisation of design, developing construction, commissioning and maintenance programme. It assumes the risk for construction performance as the equivalent of a general contractor holding all subcontracts during the construction phase. Contractors are given incentives to manage project costs by sharing cost savings.

Alliance contracting

Project owner and other alliance partners jointly develop design and share risks. Other alliance partners may include designers, consultants, management service providers, suppliers, construction contractors. It is often considered to be of greatest value where the project owner has had limited experience with the risks for the project.

Public-private partnership (PPP) and concessions

Contract between the project owner and private sector, which can reflect a number of different partnership models (e.g. Build-Operate-Transfer; Build-Own-Operate-Transfer; Design-Finance-Build-Operate-Transfer). Private sector delivers infrastructure and services over the long term with some level of private financing for the project. Payments after delivery by the private sector may be funded by government, user payments or a combination of the two. The project owner keeps control over project selection, establishes the framework conditions and retains some regulatory powers.

Table C1. Overview of private sector participation

Forms of private sector participation in infrastructure					
Characteristics	Service contract (outsourcing)	Management contract	Lease	Availability type PPPs and variations	Concession	Divestitures (privatisation)
Scope (discrete piece or network)	Discrete existing assets and network	Normally discrete existing assets	Discrete existing assets (e.g. port terminal) and networks (e.g. water)	Discrete new assets, refurbishments	Existing networks and normally existing point infrastructure (e.g. sea/ airports)	Existing network and point infrastructure (e.g. sea/ airports)
Contract duration	1-3 years	2-5 years	10-20 years	25-30 years	25-30 years	Perpetual/ subject to licence
Commercial risk for the private party	None	None	Yes	yes	Both options (yes or no)	Both options (yes or no)
Money at risk ex- ante	No	No	No	Yes	Yes	Yes
Provider of service or	Private	Private	Private	Private	Private	Private

Source: Thillairajan et al. 2013, World Bank, ADB (2008), adjusted by OECD.

ANNEX D

Country examples of infrastructure governance

Box D1. Participatory budgeting, Porto Alegre, Brazil

Participatory budgeting (PB) began more than two decades ago in Porto Alegre, the Capital of the State of Rio Grande do Sul, one of the most populous cities in South Brazil.

Participatory budgeting is a process through which citizens present their demands and priorities for civic improvement and influence the budget allocations made by their municipalities through discussions and negotiations.

Since 1989, budget allocations for public welfare works in Porto Alegre have been made only after the recommendations of public delegates and approval by the city council. The Participative Budget has proved that the democratic and transparent administration of resources is an effective way to avoid corruption and mishandling of public funds. Since its inception, the projects decided by the Participative Budget represent investments over USD 700 million, mainly in urban infrastructure.

Sources: OECD, 2016; Adapted from World Bank (2015), "Participatory budgeting in Brazil", Empowerment Case Studies, http://siteresources.worldbank.org/INTEMPOWERMENT/Resources/14657_Partic-Budg-Brazilweb.pdf; UNESCO (2015), "The experience of the participative budget in Porto Alegre, Brazil", www.unesco.org/most/southa13.htm .

Box D2. Mailing list in the Tappan Zee Bridge/I-287 Corridor Project

The Tappan Zee Bridge is located in the State of New York, crossing the Hudson River between the Village of South Nyack in Rockland County and the Village of Tarrytown in Westchester County. The project started in 2012-13 and the first span of the new twin-span bridge is scheduled to open in 2016. The new bridge should be completed in 2018.

A project mailing list, totalling more than 5 000 names and addresses, was compiled and used to distribute meeting announcements and information about the project.

Source: OECD (2015), Efficient Delivery of Large Infrastructure Projects: the Case of the New International Airport of Mexico City

---

Box D3. Public inquiry in the construction of Heathrow's Terminal 5, United Kingdom

The Construction of Heathrow Airport Terminal 5 (T5) was the largest construction project in Europe in the early 2000s. The construction of Heathrow's Terminal 5 also holds the record of the longest public inquiry in the history of the United Kingdom, which lasted nearly four years. The public inquiry cost GBP 80 million, heard 700 witnesses, and generated 100 000 pages of transcripts. The Secretary of State gave his approval to the project after reviewing the public inquiry report, and a number of conditions and limitations were imposed to take into account the complaints of local communities regarding noise and pollution.

The London Chamber of Commerce launched a campaign, Business for T5, to promote the benefits of expanding the airport. It claimed that overseas visitors would spend an estimated 10 million fewer nights in Britain if Terminal 5 did not go ahead with a loss of about GBP 1 billion to the hotels sector and another GBP 500 million to the wider tourist industry.

Box D3. Public inquiry in the construction of Heathrow's Terminal 5, United Kingdom *(cont.)*

Heathrow has since launched property and noise consultations to develop compensation packages and seek views on how that compensation fund should be used. GBP 500 million was allocated for the noise insulation and property compensation programme.

Source: Adapted from OECD (2016), Integrity Framework for Public Investment

---

Box D4. UNDP/CIPS co-operation on procurement certification

The United Nations Development Programme (UNDP) offers specialised procurement training and certification to staff from the United Nations (UN) system, non-governmental organisations, international development financing institutions and their borrowers, and governments. UNDP procurement certification courses are accredited by the Chartered Institute of Purchasing and Supply (CIPS) assuring compliance with high international qualification standards as well as offering participants access to a worldwide community of procurement professionals.

All procurement certification course content at Introductory (Level 2), Advanced (Level 3), and Diploma (Level 4) levels is tailored to reflect common United Nations and public procurement rules, policies, practices, and procedures - hereby offering a unique qualification system customised to UN and public procurement requirements. All training courses employ modern adult participatory learning methods. Each training module commences with an overview of the rules, procedures and/or theory of the subject in question, and is then followed by case studies, group discussions or exercises. This creates a forum for participants to apply theory and methods to real cases and to foster productive knowledge sharing.

Source: UNDP (n.d.), "UNDP/CIPS Cooperation on Procurement Training and Certification", www.undp.org/content/undp/en/home/operations/procurement/procurement_training.html (accessed on 20 October 2015).

Box D5. Turkey's 2002 Public Procurement Law

With the 2002 Public Procurement Law (PPL), the Public Procurement Authority (PPA) was established as an administratively and financially autonomous entity at the central governmental level to regulate and monitor public procurement. In order to prevent problems encountered previously, measures were introduced by the law to prevent pressures from interest groups and set higher ethical standards for officials, in particular:

- Members of the Public Procurement Board are appointed by the Council of Ministers and must fulfil criteria, including higher education, more than 12 years of experience in public institutions, and knowledge and experience in the field of national and international public procurement procedures. Candidates shall have no past or present relationship of membership or task with any political party. Members of the Board are nominated for a five-year term and once appointed, cannot be revoked before the expiry of their term.

- Members of the Board, except for some legally defined exceptions, cannot be involved in any official or private jobs, trade or freelance activities, and cannot be a shareholder or manager in any kind of partnerships based on commercial purposes.

Source: OECD (2007), Integrity in Public Procurement: Good Practice From A to Z, www.oecd.org/development/effectiveness/38588964.pdf, pp. 79-80.

ANNEX E

Overview of infrastructure governance dimensions

Governance Dimension	Key Policy Questions	Indicators
1. Strategic vision for infrastructure	<ul><li>Is there a whole of government vision for infrastructure investment in the medium to long term?</li><li>Is there an established process for generating, monitoring and adjusting a national strategic infrastructure vision?</li><li>Is there a dedicated unit or institution responsible for monitoring, generating, assessing, costing and creating debate around infrastructure policy?</li><li>Are there appropriate tools and processes that link the allocation of public resources to the strategic infrastructure vision?</li><li>Are strategic infrastructure plans aligned with existing spatial and land-use plans?</li><li>Is strategic infrastructure planning integrated into the spatial planning process or does it rely on independent processes?</li></ul>	<ul><li>Presence of a long term strategic plan</li><li>Strategic frameworks for public investment implementation</li><li>Budget allocation to projects in plan</li><li>Dedicated processes and units</li><li>Inter-departmental or ministerial committees and platforms to design infrastructure strategies</li></ul>
2. Manage threats to integrity	<ul><li>Are there specific measures in place in order to prevent corruption and capture from happening in infrastructure governance, such as measures to</li><li>Do audit functions have adequate capacity and resources to provide timely and reliable audits, as well as to remain insulated from manipulation of audit processes</li></ul>	<ul><li>Adequate conflict of interest policies for public officials (prohibitions of exercising certain activities or holding certain interests; post-employment measures; disclosure; advisory services) ;</li><li>System of internal controls and financial reporting to monitor and identify irregularities</li><li>Measures in place to control the integrity of firms wishing to contract with public bodies;</li><li>Mechanisms to report wrongdoing related to infrastructure projects;</li><li>Sufficient technical resources within the organisation responsible for organising public tenders;</li><li>Political contribution limits and spending limits in relation with election campaigns at national, regional and municipal levels;</li><li>Standards regulating lobbying activities and ensuring they are conducted in a transparent manner.</li></ul>

Overview of infrastructure governance dimensions *(cont.)*

Governance Dimension	Key Policy Questions	Indicators
3. Choose how to deliver infrastructure	<ul><li>What are the prioritised sectoral policy objectives?</li><li>What is the extent of market failures?</li><li>How politically sensitive is the sector?</li><li>What characterises the enabling public, private and legal environment?</li><li>What is the size and financing profile of the investment?</li><li>What is the level of control government want to retain?</li><li>What is the potential for cost recovery?</li><li>What is the level of uncertainty?</li><li>Is it possible to identify, assess and allocate risk appropriately?</li></ul>	<ul><li>Formal set of criteria to determine project prioritisation, approval and funding</li><li>Formal process or policy document to ensure value for money, for example by:<ul><li>Cost-benefit analysis</li><li>Cash flow estimates over the project cycle</li><li>Business case methodology</li></ul></li><li>Policy document and processes to ensure competitive tender process</li><li>Dedicated procedure for identifying and allocating clearly risks between public and private parties</li></ul>
4. Ensure good regulatory design	<ul><li>Is the overall regulatory framework for infrastructure sectors conducive to good governance of infrastructure,</li><li>Are there multiple layers of regulatory requirements perceived as overly burdensome?</li><li>Is there appropriate co-ordination between various regulatory bodies, as well as mechanisms for co-operation between regulators across borders?</li><li>Are the functions, powers and capacities of regulators aligned with the role of regulators in the broader infrastructure permitting and approval process?</li><li>What key data and information, including on costs of capital, asset depreciation and infrastructure consumer base, are available to inform tariff setting?</li><li>Does the overall governance of regulators facilitate confidence and trust in the infrastructure investment regime</li></ul>	<ul><li>Use of evidence-based tools for regulatory decisions<ul><li>Impact assessment</li><li>Ex-post evaluation</li></ul></li><li>Regulators<ul><li>Independence</li><li>Accountability</li><li>Sufficient scope of action</li></ul></li></ul>

Overview of infrastructure governance dimensions *(cont.)*

Governance Dimension	Key Policy Questions	Indicators
5. Consultation	• Is there an open government or consultation strategy? • Are specific stakeholder groups consulted throughout infrastructure projects phases ? • Are structured dialogue mechanisms in place to ensure systematic public consultation ? • Are there formal mechanisms to involve the public in the monitoring and implementation of infrastructure investments during the construction phase and upon completion? • Is there a forum, process or procedure for determining the balance between stakeholder interests and the public good?	• National open government strategy or guidelines (either designed for infrastructure investments or that could be applied to them) • Mapping of stakeholders • Stakeholder consultation fora or participatory budgeting programmes • Websites or other outreach tools to provide public information on infrastructure projects • Participatory auditing procedures
6. Co-ordination across levels of government	• Are the competencies related to infrastructure development allocated clearly and coherently across levels of government? • Do financing needs match the mandates granted to subnational governments for infrastructure development? • What are the main co-ordination challenges for infrastructure policy across levels of government? • What are the fiscal and policy co-ordination instruments across levels of government? • What are the governance instruments or fiscal incentives to enhance co-ordination across jurisdictions for infrastructure investment? Do they work properly?	• Formal mechanisms/bodies for co-ordination of public investment across levels of government • Co-ordination bodies/mechanisms have a multi-sector approach (across multiple ministries/departments) • Co-ordination mechanisms are frequently used and produce clear outputs/outcomes • Co-financing arrangements for infrastructure investment • Higher levels of government provide incentives for cross-jurisdictional co-ordination

Overview of infrastructure governance dimensions *(cont.)*

Governance Dimension	Key Policy Questions	Indicators
7. Affordability and Value for Money	<ul><li>Is the infrastructure procurement process integrated into the ordinary budget process?</li><li>Is the full cost of the asset budgeted upfront regardless of how it is implemented?</li><li>Is there a long term infrastructure strategy and is it linked to long term fiscal projections?</li><li>Is there a process for prioritisation across sectors and within sectors?</li><li>Is a cost-benefit analysis carried out?</li><li>Are various delivery modalities analysed so as to ensure value for money?</li><li>Is an affordability analysis carried out for the public budget and/or the users?</li><li>Are there dedicated units and capacities available to decision-makers with respect to infrastructure strategy, delivery and performance monitoring and ensuring value for money in contracting?</li><li>Are cost-benefit analyses evaluated by an institution different from the project leader?</li></ul>	<ul><li>Central Budget Authority role in green-lighting infrastructure projects</li><li>Supreme Audit Institution</li><li>PPP or Infrastructure Unit or a procurement unit in charge of infrastructures</li><li>Tests and controls to assess the maturity of the organisation responsible for delivering the project</li><li>Formal requirement to account for contingent liabilities and running costs</li><li>Formal requirement for ensuring absolute value for money</li><li>Accounting</li></ul>
8. Generation, Analysis and Disclosure of Data	<ul><li>Is there a mandatory system to ensure systematic collection of relevant financial and non- Is there a mandatory system to ensure systematic collection of relevant financial and non-financial data during the project development?</li><li>Is there a mandatory system to ensure collection of relevant financial and non-financial data about the performance of infrastructure?</li><li>Is there sufficient data that makes is possible to compare various forms of infrastructure delivery models? Are they compared based on data?</li><li>Is financial and non-financial data about the project (*ex ante* and performance) disclosed to the public?</li></ul>	<ul><li>Central unit (Central Infrastructure Unit, Central Budget Authority) for the collection, disclosure and analysis of data.</li><li>Choice of delivery modality and projects is based on data.</li><li>Key Performance Indicators to assess infrastructure performance</li><li>Disclosure of data in an open format on a dedicated website</li><li>Infrastructure investment flow data (in sectorial breakdown)</li><li>Infrastructure investment stock data (in sectorial breakdown)</li></ul>

Overview of infrastructure governance dimensions *(cont.)*

Governance Dimension	Key Policy Questions	Indicators
9. Performance throughout the life-cycle	• Is there a strategy for how performance of the asset throughout the life of the asset is to be ensured? • Do relevant line ministry or agency conduct performance assessment and monitoring of each project? Are there programmes in place for training and capacitating relevant institutions? • Do PPP/concession/procurement contracts state the required output and performance? • Is there a strategy in case of renegotiations?	• Policy document for ensuring performance from assets regulated by agency (sector regulator) or by contract with line department or similar. • Clear remit of the sectorial ministries and authorities to develop, assess and monitor infrastructure policy and performance • Strategy for re-negotiations. • Ex-post evaluation of value for money.
10. Systemic risks	• Are there policies in place to ensure that key infrastructure assets are resilient if disasters hit? • Are key structures designing to sustain a foreseeable shock or are substitute or redundant systems available. • Is there management capacity to identify options, prioritising actions, and communicate decisions to the people who will implement them? • Are there tools in place to learn from past events?	• The presence of a disaster risk assessment plan • The presence of designated authorities responsible for tackling disasters

ORGANISATION FOR ECONOMIC CO-OPERATION AND DEVELOPMENT

OECD PUBLISHING, 2, rue André-Pascal, 75775 PARIS CEDEX 16

(42 2017 15 1 P) ISBN 978-92-64-27244-6 – 2017